T0339622

Workplace Safety
ESTABLISHING AN EFFECTIVE VIOLENCE PREVENTION PROGRAM

Workplace Safety
ESTABLISHING AN EFFECTIVE VIOLENCE PREVENTION PROGRAM

RANDALL W. FERRIS

DANIEL MURPHY

ELSEVIER

Amsterdam • Boston • Heidelberg • London
New York • Oxford • Paris • San Diego
San Francisco • Singapore • Sydney • Tokyo
Butterworth-Heinemann is an imprint of Elsevier

Acquiring Editor: Tom Stover
Editorial Project Manager: Hilary Carr
Project Manager: Priya Kumaraguruparan
Cover Designer: Greg Harris

Butterworth-Heinemann is an imprint of Elsevier
The Boulevard, Langford Lane, Kidlington, Oxford OX5 1GB, UK
225 Wyman Street, Waltham, MA 02451, USA

Copyright © 2016 Elsevier Inc. All rights reserved.

No part of this publication may be reproduced or transmitted in any form or by any means, electronic or mechanical, including photocopying, recording, or any information storage and retrieval system, without permission in writing from the publisher. Details on how to seek permission, further information about the Publisher's permissions policies and our arrangements with organizations such as the Copyright Clearance Center and the Copyright Licensing Agency, can be found at our website: www.elsevier.com/permissions.

This book and the individual contributions contained in it are protected under copyright by the Publisher (other than as may be noted herein).

Notices
Knowledge and best practice in this field are constantly changing. As new research and experience broaden our understanding, changes in research methods, professional practices, or medical treatment may become necessary.

Practitioners and researchers must always rely on their own experience and knowledge in evaluating and using any information, methods, compounds, or experiments described herein. In using such information or methods they should be mindful of their own safety and the safety of others, including parties for whom they have a professional responsibility.

To the fullest extent of the law, neither the Publisher nor the authors, contributors, or editors, assume any liability for any injury and/or damage to persons or property as a matter of products liability, negligence or otherwise, or from any use or operation of any methods, products, instructions, or ideas contained in the material herein.

British Library Cataloguing-in-Publication Data
A catalogue record for this book is available from the British Library

Library of Congress Cataloging-in-Publication Data
A catalog record for this book is available from the Library of Congress

ISBN: 978-0-12-802775-2

For information on all Butterworth-Heinemann publications
visit our website at http://store.elsevier.com/

Working together
to grow libraries in
developing countries

ELSEVIER | Book Aid International

www.elsevier.com • www.bookaid.org

CONTENTS

FOREWORD

RANDY

My introduction to violence came in 1962 when I was six years old. It arrived via a television drama called *Combat!* This weekly one-hour series ran until 1967 and followed a U.S. Army infantry squad as they advanced through France during World War II. It starred Vic Morrow and Rick Jansen with a cast of recurring characters portrayed by a host of different actors, including silent screen heartthrob Ramon Navarro, comedians Shecky Greene and Jack Carter, future Academy Award winner Robert Duvall, and Leonard Nimoy and Walter Koenig, before they attained starring roles on *Star Trek*. The violence on *Combat!* was glorious, courageous, and noble, as good triumphed over evil. My childhood buddies and I reenacted scenes in the woods behind our homes, complete with authentic plastic helmets and weapons manufactured by the Mattel toy company.

My introduction to real violence came three years later in 1964. It arrived via an alcoholic, abusive father. We were living above the means of his teacher's salary, so he took a second job playing the piano in taverns. He began drinking when he was in the eighth grade, and in college he graduated to liquor and participated in promiscuous sexual activity. He did begin to settle into harmonious family life until he began working five to six nights a week in various bars where the liquor flowed and promiscuous sex was readily available. When the abuse started, it was generally aimed toward my mother, but eventually my older sister and I were caught in the crosshairs. You can put any modifier you want next to the word "abuse" and it eventually visited our family: verbal abuse, physical abuse, and etcetera. Unlike in the TV show, *Combat!*, this violence was horrific, cowardly, and dishonorable. The truly terrifying portions of the abuse normally took place when my father came home from the bar. To this day I still awaken every night between midnight and 1:00 a.m., as this was usually when he came home. I could tell from the way he closed the door whether or not I could go back to sleep or curl up in the fetal position as the "fight or flight" physiological responses coursed through my body. During the day I became an expert in assessing his behaviors, which let me know if it was safe to interact with him, or whether I should give him a wide berth. Dinnertime was the second most frequent occurrence of abuse, usually in its verbal format. We never knew which father would be joining us at the table—the charming, gregarious dad or the malicious, vindictive father. When I assessed that it was the latter, I attempted, sometimes successfully and sometimes unsuccessfully, to de-escalate the tension through humor or by diverting the conversation to something I knew was a safer topic.

Although these were not pleasant childhood experiences, they did wise me up fast. Alcoholics develop a talent for deception and manipulation, and learning to see through those traits served me well throughout my career in corporate security.

DAN

As fate would have it, I was raised in a working-class neighborhood in western Queens that bordered both the Long Island City and Sunnyside sections of the borough. The majority of the men in that area were construction workers and tradesmen, or some other version of blue-collar worker: police officers, sanitation workers, or other civil servants, like my father, a Transit Authority electrical worker. New York City at that time, which was the late 1960s and 1970s, was awash in crime and violence. It was not uncommon to see junkies gather in one of the local concrete schoolyards at night to use drugs. It also was not uncommon to be the victim of some form of violence, whether that was in a schoolyard fight with a classmate or while riding the ever-dangerous New York City subway system. I recall seeing more than one homicide victim on the streets and witnessing the police response and media attention that naturally follows such a discovery. I was mugged at age 13 and my sister was assaulted by a gang while on her way home from high school, both while on the subway. I also recall our home being burglarized when I was a child. Perhaps the most memorable violence-related event was the night that the police interrupted our slumber to follow a blood trail up the stairs to the small second-floor apartment my father rented to two fledgling Mafia members. The wannabe mobsters had already grabbed what they wanted and fled into the night. The next day, they were machine-gunned to death in a gas station—so it went back then in that place. Violence was all around me, including in my home where my older brother Jim and I used to spar with each other over the slightest of transgressions. More than one of these fights resulted in broken walls, furniture, and bones. My former Marine father was not amused. I look back now and think that the Ali–Frazier fights were nothing in comparison to my brother and me.

Despite my upbringing and familiarity with violence, I was still unprepared for what I would see and deal with on joining the New York Police Department in 1984 at the age of 21. My eyes were opened widely to the brutal violence that seemed to be a daily occurence in the poverty-, drug-, and desperation-filled neighborhoods in which I would work during my 20-year career.

As any experienced street cop or detective knows, you frequently come into contact with people moving toward violence. As such, and in an effort to minimize the number of fights and physical altercations you have to engage in, you develop an ability to de-escalate the violent person. This is an art that is learned by watching more experienced officers handle such people. Once you learn how to do this, it is the equivalent of a master's degree in psychology. I found this skill to be invaluable when dealing with potentially violent people in my corporate and consulting roles.

In time I began to see past the act and its aftermath and to learn to focus on what was behind the violence. To be a successful police detective, you must understand human beings and what makes them do what they do to each other. What causes a person to take another person's life or torture, strangle, rape, and abuse another human being? I soon saw that it was a variety of things, but most of it had to do with external influences. I truly believe that almost no one is a born killer, but that a lifetime of abuse and violence can form a person to act out violently with no hesitation. I also have seen countless cases where the only motivator was greed. The most curious to me, however, were the unfortunate souls who could not contain their emotions, caused by broken hearts or jealous streaks, and flew into rages, causing death and destruction. Theirs was a temporary mental condition with lifelong repercussions—a permanent and terribly incorrect answer to a temporary problem.

PREFACE

This book has been written for the practitioner – the peacekeeper or referee – within an organization. In other words this book was written for the person who is responsible for the safety and security of the associates as well as the guests. You may come from many different disciplines, such as loss prevention, risk management, security, safety, human resources, employee relations, operations management, facilities management, and so forth. We welcome you all, we share the anxiety you have about being responsible for the lives of the people within your facility, and we applaud you for your decision to learn about violence prevention and how to apply it within your organization. The anxiety you feel will greatly dissipate once you have a viable violence prevention plan in place.

This book was written for your benefit. Our tome is not an in-depth psychological study of those who have become ordained in violence, although there will be succinct discussions of the motivations and symptoms of those who engage in threats, harassment, assaults, and rampage-driven homicide.

We entered this endeavor with two guiding principles: (1) to give you the tools you need to get a violence prevention plan up and running and (2) to provide concise and impactful information that is backed up by facts and just enough case studies to prove our points.

The information contained herein is presented in 12 chapters sectioned into three parts. Part I is entitled "Getting Your Ducks in a Row" and contains three chapters:

1. Definitions, Statistics, and the Occupational Safety and Health Administration
2. The Need for a Violence Prevention Plan
3. Overcoming Rationalizations, Objections, and Denials

This part provides the evidence you need to prove your case for a violence prevention plan and gives you the tools to overcome the roadblocks that might be thrown in your way. Part II, entitled "Getting Everyone Up-to-Speed," contains the next four chapters:

4. The Root Sources of Workplace Violence
5. Relationship Violence
6. Employee Violence
7. External Violence

These chapters discuss the real risks and the likelihood of you having to face them. Part II also contains the symptomatic behaviors indicative of someone who is troubled and may be moving toward violence.

Part III, entitled "Formulating a Plan and Putting It Into Action," comprises the final four chapters of the book:

8. The Seven Components of a Comprehensive Violence Prevention Plan

9. Staff and Management Training

10. Putting Together Your Situational Assessment and Management Team

11. Managing Threats and Disturbing Behavior

12. Managing the Aftermath of Violence

Part III lays out sample violence prevention plan, the training components for your staff and management teams, and how to put together a situational assessment and management team. Finally, this section takes you through the intricacies of building threat management plans and gives you an in-depth look at managing the aftermath of violence.

It was our deliberate plan to produce a book that was concise and impactful so that you can gain an understanding of the concepts quickly. We know that some readers may read the chapters out of order or skip others entirely as they want to get to the topics that cover the most pressing issues for their organization. As such, we will occasionally repeat information from prior chapters or refer the reader to a previous section when there is important information that precedes a new topic.

The primary market for this book is businesses and as such, we tend to use the words "business" and "employee" quite frequently. However, the concepts presented herein can also be applied to schools, houses of worship, healthcare facilities, nonprofit organizations, shopping malls, or other places where people come together and interact, even a household. Because of this, we also intermittently use the words "organization" and "associate."

We hope you find this book easy to digest, and we know that the information contained in the upcoming chapters will be helpful in protecting the employees and associates in your business or organization. Be alert, be responsive, and be safe.

ABOUT THE AUTHORS

RANDALL W. FERRIS

Randy Ferris spent 31 years in proprietary security working for several large organizations. In 1996, after having to deal with three serious incidents involving domestic and workplace violence, he began searching for methods by which his company could identify situations that had the potential to become violent and mitigate them before a serious incident occurred. After conducting his own independent research and receiving training from several nationally renowned experts, he put together violence prevention programs for three Fortune 100 companies.

Since then Randy has provided training for a number of large organizations and helped them develop policies & processes related to violence prevention, violence response, and the aftermath of violence. He is also a sought after speaker and has addressed various subjects related to domestic and workplace violence for the Minnesota Crime Prevention Association, the Food Marketing Institute's Risk Management Conference, and the International Association of Financial Crimes Investigators.

Randy is also a proud member of the Association of Threat Assessment Professionals.

Randy Ferris and Dan Murphy can be contacted through their website, www.violencepreventionstrategies.org for:
- Speaking engagements
- Assistance in the development of training, policies and processes
- Assessment of a current threat
- Assistance developing threat management plans
- Other requests as appropriate

DANIEL MURPHY, M.A., CFE, CFCI

Dan Murphy is a retired Detective-Sergeant from the New York City Police Department, where he served for twenty years. His accomplishments there include 16 years as either a Detective or Detective-Sergeant serving in units such as the Narcotics Division, the Organized Crime Investigation Division, the Major Case Squad, the Bronx Gang Investigations Squad, and ultimately the Joint Terrorism Task Force (JTTF), after 9-11. His areas of expertise included Federal RICO investigations of violent gangs, kidnapping, human trafficking, bank robbery, and counterterrorism.

Dan has received numerous awards for outstanding patrol and detective work, including the 2003 National Association of Police Organizations (NAPO) TOP COP Award, given by John Walsh of "America's Most Wanted" in Washington, DC.

Dan was a first responder to the terror attacks of both February 26, 1993, and September 11, 2001 on the World Trade Center. He has also performed undercover work in Southeast Asia while working in a task force with the U.S. Drug Enforcement Administration.

After leaving the NYPD Dan worked for The Bank of New York as a Financial Crimes and Fraud Investigator, targeting possible terrorist financing schemes. He then spent eight years with Albertson's/Supervalu as Director of Corporate, Supply Chain, and Global Security and Investigations. He is also Founding Partner of Violence Prevention Strategies LLC, and was an Associate Director in the Compliance and Privacy Investigations Areas of Optum Health. He currently is the Chief Security Officer for a large financial institution.

Dan has a Bachelor of Arts Degree in Criminal Justice from the John Jay College of Criminal Justice in New York City, and a Master of Arts in Public Safety Administration from St. Mary's University of Minnesota where he is a member of the Adjunct Faculty teaching classes on Workplace Violence Prevention, Private Investigations Techniques, and the Graduate level Capstone program.

His professional affiliations include the American Society for Industrial Security (ASIS), the Association of Threat Assessment Professionals (ATAP), and the Association of Certified Fraud Examiners (ACFE), the International Association of Financial Crimes Investigators (IAFCI), the International Security Management Association (ISMA), and the Overseas Security Advisory Committee (OSAC) of the U.S. Department of State.

Dan is a Certified Fraud Examiner (CFE), and a Certified Financial Crimes Investigator (CFCI).

ACKNOWLEDGMENTS

RANDY

In any body of work on a subject so complex as workplace safety and violence prevention, there is a great deal of passion, experience, training, and practice that germinates over a long period of time before pen ever meets paper. As such, there is a long list of people to acknowledge and thank.

First and foremost is Gavin de Becker, whose seminal work, *The Gift of Fear*, first lit my passion and made me realize that there were better methods to respond to threats than the ones I had previously employed. His book and his training seminars have given me a broader understanding in assessing and managing threats and have undoubtedly saved lives. My most sincere thanks go to this man. I would also like to thank Gavin de Becker's many associates both past and present. Bob Martin, Ellen Prystajko, Gabrielle Thompson, Matt Slatoff, and Dave Falconer, who have all been generous with their time and knowledge whether in training sessions or case consultations. I am forever indebted to Gavin de Becker and his associates.

Another huge influence is Lt. Col. David Grossman. His encouragement, spirited training sessions, and insight into the threat of terrorism and personal awareness and preparation are enlightening and inspirational. His book, *On Killing: The Psychological Cost of Learning to Kill in War and Society*, is another "must read" for anyone interested in understanding the psychology of violence. Readers should also peruse his website, www.killology.com, to review his resources and see when he may be speaking in your area. Attending one of his seminars is time and money very well spent.

I would also like to thank Peter Bartholomew, Mike DePaola, and Carol Martinson. All were former "bosses" who encouraged my study and gave the "go ahead" for many of the training programs I attended. I should also note John Sims and Todd Sheldon, two corporate counsels who understood the methods that my partner Dan Murphy and I employed and trusted us implicitly. Special thanks goes to Beth Nuccio, who taught me the how and why of business investigations, and to my first "boss" Ron Green, who taught me that the key to being a good investigator was to treat people as you would want to be treated if you were under similar circumstances. Similar thanks go to Doug Wicklander and Dave Zulawski, who taught many of us in corporate security how to detect deception and remove the barriers that suppress the truth.

I must also acknowledge the team of associates I have worked with in the past: Tracy, Doug, Kelly, Joe D., Mike, Randy (a different Randy, not me), Dave, and Joey C., who had a continual penchant for calling me on Fridays at 4:45 p.m. with a new and complex challenge.

I would certainly be remiss if I did not also thank my business partner Dan Murphy, who coined the name of our business, Violence Prevention Strategies, LLC, and who has constantly challenged and pushed our company to continually find new ways to serve our clients and community.

Finally, I want to thank my wonderful daughters for being who they are. You are always in the back of my mind and the forefront of my heart in everything I do. I love you so very much.

DAN

Years of dealing with violence after the damage had been done did not prepare me for what I would have to learn to deal with in a corporate setting. After retiring from the New York Police Department (NYPD), I was fortunate enough to land a position with Albertson's in Boise, Idaho. Although I thought of myself as someone who understood people, I soon learned that I had much to learn indeed about managing and assessing the threat posed by people often within my organization. I thought too much like a cop and wanted everyone arrested, thinking "that would take care of that," so to say. My approach needed redirection, and for that I will always be grateful to Randy. He introduced me to the world of threat assessment and management. I learned so much by working with him on countless cases of threatening, stalking, and harassing behavior perpetrated by both our employees and by external persons associated with them. It was from here that I first attended the Gavin de Becker Threat Assessment and Management Academy in the hills above Los Angeles, where my thinking truly began shifting in the right direction. I credit the excellent de Becker team with helping me learn volumes about human aggression and the best methods to employ to de-escalate a situation. Among those fine people were Bob Martin, whose wisdom, friendship, and experience always amazes me; and Matt Slatoff and Ellen Prystajko, who both are among the best at what they do. Another de Becker Academy benefit was meeting retired U.S. Army Lt. Col. David Grossman, and hearing him speak about violence and killing. He is, perhaps, the most compelling speaker I have ever seen. I have devoured his books and recommend all who study human aggression to follow suit. No one looks at the subject the same way after hearing Lt. Col. Grossman speak.

I would be remiss if I did not mention some of the many incredible people with whom I had the honor of working and facing down violence daily while with the NYPD. I learned more about life and death from them than most people ever will. I want to thank Bob Metcalfe, with whom I grew up and who was my real first partner—gutsy, tough, and street-smart with a quick smile and laugh. I want to thank other 30th Precinct friends: Donny Rogers, Eddie O'Dea, Ed Connolly, and Jimmy Henry, who left us far too young and tragically—may you be at peace now Jimmy. I want to thank John Walsh with whom I handled and faced serious violence almost every night in Washington Heights in the1980s, yet we always managed to laugh. I also want to acknowledge Joe Barbato and Mike Buczek (rest in peace, Michael), who both fearlessly worked the mean streets of the Heights back in the day; Joe Gallagher with whom I would embark on a daily voyage in search of wanted fugitives for two years; Bill Walsh, my brother in arms in Brooklyn North Narcotics in the days when homicides were a daily, if not hourly occurrence in that stretch of real estate; my entire team at OCID-Al Goohs—JJ Kelly, Ray Polanco, Jimmy O'Connor, Louie B., Brigid Faenza, Keith Adkins (DEA), with whom I performed a dangerous undercover assignment in Hong Kong— all exceptional people and talented investigators. I learned so much from you all and from the Major Case Squad, Bob Sassok, who is the ultimate cop and detective who does everything the best—thank you for teaching me how to be a squad detective. Thanks to John O'Boyle, my brother from another mother and the best partner I could ever ask for. Not only is he an amazing investigator, but the most fun anyone will ever have legally is to work with him! Thanks to Tom Nerney, the quintessential NYPD Detective; if Tommy doesn't know it, it's not worth knowing. To Paul Helbock, Mike Hines, Pete Tartaglia, Bill Oldham, Jack Ryan, Joe Piraino, Greg White, Ruben Santiago, and countless others, thank you for teaching me how to walk, talk, think, and act like a detective. I looked up to you all and still do. To my friends and partners from the 46th Precinct, I valued your bravery and work ethic more than you can imagine; you are great cops working in a crime-infested, violent area. Rest in peace, Sergio Villanueva, formerly of the 46th Precinct, who died at the World Trade Center on September 11, 2001, as a Fire Department of New York member. You were a great street cop and gentle, brave soul and will always be missed. Thanks to the Bronx Gang Squad—Tommy Smith, John Bottone, and John Keeley—superb, dogged investigators. Adios OG Mack! Among the many others bearing mention and thanks are Timmy Breen, Patty Morena, Scott Curcio, Danny O'Brien, who could all make the Pope laugh during a high mass; John Asam and the entire team at TARU, true professionals; everyone at the Joint Terrorism Task Force (JTTF) in New York, including my partner, FBI Supervisory Special Agent Dave Shafer, simply the best to work with. It was an honor Dave. To the many, many fine people who I was privileged to have worked with and shared so many incredible experiences, good and bad while with the NYPD, I say that words aren't enough. You had my back and I had yours and that will always unite us. Thank you; remember 9-11, and our brothers and sisters who gave their lives that day.

To the people who influenced me greatly and molded me into a corporate security professional: Mike DePaola, who took me under his wing and taught me so much I can't express it properly here; my partner, Randy Ferris without his guidance, friendship, and tutelage I would not have learned about this subject at all; Red Burke, a fellow former NYPD Detective, who made my landing at the Bank of New York a soft one, my entire team at Albertson's SuperValu; Michael Royce, Joe Holmes, Bill Smithey, Ryan Casey and Ben Paulin, true professionals and friends; and last but not least, Carol Martinson, who seemingly made it her life's mission to develop me in all areas so that I would become a true professional despite my cop tendencies! Thank you Carol for standing by me and believing in me through some very rough times. I will never forget your support!

I also want to thank my wonderful family without whom I am and have nothing. To my father, James, who was taken far too soon, thank you for teaching me how to be a man. I hope to see you on the other side. To my incredible mom, Kathleen (Kitty), without her loving hand I would not have made it through so much of my life. To my tremendous sister Maureen, and brother James (NYPD Detective-Sergeant Retired), your love and endless support have always given me strength. I love you both. To my beautiful children, Erin and Daniel, words fail me as I attempt to say how much you both mean to me. I will love you to the grave and beyond. You inspire me daily to be better in every way as you both are.

Last, I want to thank my beautiful wife, Angela Lyn. Your love and support has been unwavering throughout this project. Thank you for your encouragement and for reading pieces to keep me on track. It's meant the world to me. You have my heart always.

We would both like to thank the team at Elsevier for their confidence and encouragement in the preparation of this book. Special thanks to our Editorial Project Manager Hilary Carr for answering our questions, holding our hands (telephonically), finding solutions to problems, and cutting us a break when we needed one. None of this would have been possible without their help.

PART I

Getting Your Ducks in a Row

CHAPTER 1

Definitions, Statistics, and the Occupational Safety and Health Administration

"You see, but you do not observe. The distinction is clear."
—*Sir Arthur Conan Doyle,* **The Adventures of Sherlock Holmes** *(1892)*

Contents

Abstract

Any work that discusses workplace violence must first include a solid, universally accepted set of definitions. Chapter 1 defines workplace violence using the Occupational Safety and Health Administration (OSHA)-enhanced definition, which includes not only actual violence but threatening, harassing, stalking, and disturbing behavior. It also includes a look at workplace violence statistics, such as the more than 2 million official complaints lodged annually by U.S. workers for violations of the OSHA definition. This chapter also extensively discusses OSHA's role in investigating and reporting these events, as well as how OSHA handles such reports and what they will expect from employers. The chapter concludes with a look at the actual monetary fines levied by OSHA in cases where an employer failed to provide and maintain a safe, secure working environment for their employees. Additionally, this chapter shows how the Uniform Crime Report of the Federal Bureau of Investigation (FBI) fails to collect data and report on workplace violence cases despite being continually updated to include new crime categories.

Keywords: Federal Bureau of Investigation (FBI); employees; fines; hazards; lawsuits; National Institute for Occupational Safety and Health (NIOSH); Occupational Safety and Health Administration (OSHA); safety; threats; Uniform Crime Report (UCR); workplace violence

Amanda Brown was dead. The notification call came early in the morning. Amanda was dead and she was dead for two reasons; to the horror of coworkers and guests, her estranged husband stabbed her more than 20 times while she was working with clients. The other reason she was dead was because Amanda, her coworkers, and supervisors did not recognize that her estranged husband's behavior was escalating and did not piece together that the legal actions she had just completed would cause her husband to boil over in homicidal rage.

Amanda's story is all too familiar in the United States. She met her husband when they both worked for the same company. They fell in love and got married. Shortly after their marriage, his behavior turned sour. He had always been somewhat jealous and somewhat controlling, but after the marriage this behavior escalated and he frequently falsely accused her of cheating on him. He kept her from seeing her friends or having any life outside of work and home. He began to exhibit behaviors consistent with paranoia and his actions turned abusive: first verbally and emotionally and then physically. His disturbing behavior eventually began to spill over to the workplace. He was a contracted employee from another organization working at Amanda's company and her employer soon asked that he be replaced.

Meanwhile, their home life continued to deteriorate. Eventually Amanda had enough and left him. After she moved out, he occasionally would harass and physically assault her in the parking lot of her apartment or in her company's parking lot. This caused her company to transfer her to another location.

However, he quickly found out about her new work location and the periodic assaults continued. She applied for and received a temporary restraining order and while it provided her with a slight respite from his abuse, it did not completely reform his behavior. After several months Amanda decided to take further action. She found a new apartment and did not tell anyone where she was moving. She took vacation time to move and unpack. On her second-to-last day off she went back to court and requested that the temporary restraining order be made permanent. The request was granted. Afterward she stopped by her place of employment to notify them of her new address and provide them with a copy of the restraining order. On the following day Amanda was taking care of a few odds and ends related to her relocation while her estranged husband was being served with the new, permanent restraining order. He immediately and repeatedly began calling her place of employment and was continually told that she was not there.

On the following day Amanda returned to work and was told about the prior day's phone calls from her husband. She let everyone know that if he called today she would not talk to him. He did begin to call but this day instead of being told that she was not there, he was informed that she did not want to talk to him. Soon he stopped calling and showed up in person with his knife.

It is unfair to look at this tragic murder months later when all the pieces of the puzzle are revealed and all of the facts are known and wonder why no one saw the danger coming as easily as we can recognize it now. We have the benefit of knowing all of the facts but at the time, no one person knew everything that had happened. Amanda thought the restraining order would protect her, but restraining orders are largely prosecutorial tools, not bulletproof (or in this instance knife-proof) shields. Also Amanda, her coworkers and supervisors were not experts in personal security nor were they trained to assess threats. Because there was no repository of all of the facts and there was no one trained to assess them as a bigger picture, the events that occurred were viewed as individual, unconnected incidents. Yes, Amanda's horrific death could have been prevented but only if the organization had trained their people to recognize distinct behaviors; only if the organization had given their people a process whereby they could report their concerns; and only if the organization had a team trained to investigate the concerns, assess the behaviors, and develop effective plans to deescalate threats and mitigate risks. And that is exactly what you will learn in this book.

WORKPLACE VIOLENCE IS NOT A CRIME

There is no statute declaring that workplace violence is a criminal violation of the law. The actions that are commonly associated with workplace violence are prosecuted under a variety of laws related to making threats, committing intimidation or harassment, malicious vandalism, criminal damage to property, stalking, domestic violence, assaults, and homicide. The problem for those studying workplace violence is twofold:

1. There is no statutory definition of workplace violence.
2. There is difficulty in assembling accurate statistical data related to the arrests and prosecutions of workplace violence as not every commission of threatening behavior, intimidation, harassment, vandalism, damage to property, stalking, domestic violence, assaults, or homicide is related to workplace violence.

REPORTING AT THE FEDERAL LEVEL

After much study in the 1920s, the Federal Bureau of Investigation (FBI) instituted the Uniform Crime Report in 1929. The Uniform Crime Report (UCR) is a database of local, state, tribal, and federal law enforcement statistics. The report details the number of incidents, offenses, victims, and offenders in three principle categories [1]:

1. Crimes against persons, which include
   a. Assault
   b. Homicide
   c. Kidnapping
   d. Forcible sex offenses, and
   e. Non-forcible sex offenses
2. Crimes against property, which include
   a. Arson
   b. Bribery
   c. Burglary
   d. Counterfeiting
   e. Destruction
   f. Embezzlement
   g. Extortion
   h. Fraud
   i. Theft
   j. Motor vehicle theft

    k. Robbery
    l. Stolen property
3. Crimes against Society, which include
    a. Drug offenses
    b. Gambling
    c. Pornography
    d. Prostitution
    e. Weapons violations

Workplace and its intertwined offense of domestic violence are nowhere to be found. As was illustrated in the death of Amanda Brown, many instances of workplace violence are the result of domestic violence that spills over onto the job site, so the two issues are very closely related.

The FBI's UCR breaks out sex offenses into two categories: forcible and non-forcible. Theft of material and financial property are expanded to seven line items: burglary, embezzlement, fraud, theft, motor vehicle theft, robbery, and stolen property. But workplace violence is nowhere to be found within the report. And, on September 17, 2014, FBI director James B. Comey announced that the FBI would add cruelty to animals to the national UCR program as a unique category of offense to be reported in the "Crimes against Society" section. [2] But workplace and domestic violence are nowhere to be found within the "Crimes against Persons" category.

While there is no law enforcement repository of workplace violence definitions and statistics, there is a federal regulatory body in the United States that collects data and investigates an organization's state of preparedness (and assesses fines for a lack thereof), which is the Department of Labor's Occupational Safety and Health Administration, more commonly referred to as OSHA. OSHA defines workplace violence as follows: "Workplace violence is any act or threat of physical violence, harassment, intimidation, or other threatening disruptive behavior that occurs at the work site. It ranges from threats and verbal abuse to physical assaults and even homicide." [3]

The FBI's UCR for 2012 (the last year available at the time of this writing) shows that there were 1,214,462 instances of crimes against persons (assaults, homicides, kidnappings, and sex offenses) in the United States. [4] Perhaps there are just not enough occurrences of workplace violence to justify breaking it out into its own line item on the UCR. However, OSHA's website reports that "nearly 2 million American workers report having been victims of workplace violence each year. Unfortunately, many more cases go unreported. The truth is, workplace violence can strike anywhere, anytime, and no one is immune." [5] Clearly there is a gap between the data reported by the FBI and OSHA. Let's clear up at least some of the disparity:

- The FBI's UCR shows arrests whereas OSHA's data includes everything reported to OSHA and many of those incidents are handled within the reporting business without anyone being arrested or without any notification to the police.
- The FBI's UCR details arrests for physical crimes against persons (assault, homicide, etc.) whereas OSHA is cataloging all incidents reported to them of physical violence, harassment, intimidation, threats, and verbal abuse. Therefore OSHA is collecting data from a larger pool of incidents than is reported and included in the FBI's report.
- There are those who dismiss OSHA's statistics stating that OSHA's workplace violence data is inflated because it also includes other violations of the law in which a worker may be placed in danger, such as robbery, which is captured in the "Crimes against Property" section of the UCR. However, most all business robberies are reported to the police and this category has not reached 100,000 incidents in each of the UCR for the last two years. [6] Therefore the number of robberies in the United States is not causing statistically significant inflation in the workplace violence data reported by OSHA.

According to the FBI, the goal of the UCR is to "generate reliable information for law enforcement administration, operation and management" as well as to detect emerging social trends in criminal or other antisocial behavior. [7] In that regard it would be beneficial to know how many of those arrests for assaults and homicides were related to workplace and domestic violence so that the proper social, legislative, and law enforcement resources could be marshaled against this trend. This should not be difficult as it would be a programming change to the reporting police department's existing computerized reporting system, asking the arresting officer if the offense being reported involved workplace or domestic violence.

OSHA'S ROLE

The Occupational Safety and Health Act was signed into law on December 29, 1970, and established the Occupation Safety and Health Administration as a part of the U.S. Department of Labor. OSHA's mission is to "assure safe and healthful working conditions for working men and women by setting and enforcing standards and by providing training, outreach, education and assistance." OSHA [8] also has the duty to enforce a variety of whistleblower statues and regulations and protect workers that have made a claim to the agency from retaliation by employers or other employees.

Although OSHA currently has no specific standards for the prevention of workplace violence, it is covered under the General Duty Clause, Section 5(a)(1) of the Occupational Safety and Health Act of 1970. [9] This section of the General Duty Clause states that employers must provide their employees with a workplace that is "free from recognizable hazards that are causing or likely to cause death or serious harm to employees." Therefore by applying OSHA's definition of workplace violence any business, institution, or organization that has experienced any act or threat of physical violence, harassment, intimidation, or other threatening disruptive behavior is on notice that there is a risk of serious harm or death to their employees and needs to implement a comprehensive workplace violence prevention program, including the implementation of physical controls within their work environment, training of their employees, and security measures appropriate to the level of the threat.

Further, OSHA protects employees from retaliation via Section 11(c)(1) and (2) of the General Duty Clause, which states:

No person shall discharge or in any manner discriminate against any employee because such employee has filed any complaint or instituted or caused to be instituted any proceeding under or related to this Act or has testified or is about to testify in any such proceeding or because of the exercise by such employee on behalf of himself or others of any right afforded by this Act.

Any employee who believes that he has been discharged or otherwise discriminated against by any person in violation of this subsection may, within thirty days after such violation occurs, file a complaint with the Secretary alleging such discrimination. Upon receipt of such complaint, the Secretary shall cause such investigation to be made as he deems appropriate. If upon such investigation, the Secretary determines that the provisions of this subsection have been violated, he shall bring an action in any appropriate United States district court against such person. In any such action the United States district courts shall have jurisdiction, for cause shown to restrain violations … and order all appropriate relief including rehiring or reinstatement of the employee to his former position with back pay. [10]

OSHA's Involvement in Workplace Violence

In 2011 OSHA issued instructions to its compliance officers titled "Enforcement Procedures for Investigating or Inspecting Workplace Violence

Incidents." OSHA instructs its officers to initiate workplace violence inspections when "(1) responding to a complaint, referral, or a fatality or catastrophic event; and (2) conducting a programmed inspection where workplace violence is identified as an issue." [11] A programmed inspection refers to any scheduled inspection whether routine or in response to a complaint. The inspection would include workplace violence if the location fits the risk factors explained later in the next section or if the subject of workplace violence is identified during the routine inspection.

These instructions also break out workplace violence into four distinct, but fairly self-explanatory, categories:

1. "Criminal Intent," which OSHA defines as "violent acts by people who enter the workplace to commit a robbery or other crime..."

2. "Customer/Client/Patients" is defined as "violence directed at employees by customers, clients, patients, students,k inmates or any others to whom the employer provides a service."

3. "Co-Worker" is described as "violence against co-workers, supervisors, or managers by a current or former employee, supervisor, or manager.

4. "Personal" is defined as "violence in the workplace by someone who does not work there, but who is known to, or has a personal relationship with an employee."

OSHA WORKPLACE VIOLENCE INSPECTIONS

As per their 2011 instruction to their officers (OSHA Directive Number CPL 02-01-052), here is what the OSHA officer will request or otherwise want to ascertain during their inspection:

- Review all incident reports concerning issues of workplace violence.
- Identify and interview all employees in charge of security and/or have responsibility for the workplace violence prevention program.
- Review the workplace violence prevention program to determine if the employer has implemented appropriate controls for work protection, including training, physical controls over the premises, secure work practices, and personal protective equipment (such as personal *panic* alarms), disciplinary records related to violence or aggression shown in the workplace, medical records related to workplace violence, police reports, and actions taken to prevent future acts of workplace violence.
- Identify jobs or locations with the greatest potential for workplace violence, as well as any processes and procedures that put workers at risk, including building layout, interior and exterior lighting, communication systems, and the absence of appropriate security systems.
- Interview all employees on all shifts who observed or experienced any acts of workplace violence.
- Interview first responders, police officers, managers, and any others who observed the incident or its aftermath.

If a serious workplace violence hazard is found to exist, the OSHA inspector will also be looking for the following:

- OSHA 300 (Injury/Illness) logs and 301 forms documenting injuries from workplace violence for the prior five years
- Injury reports specific to instances of workplace violence
- Past complaints or grievances noting the particular hazard
- Meeting minutes where workplace violence issues were discussed
- Workers' compensation records documenting injuries from workplace violence
- Medical records regarding workplace violence incidents
- Police and security records documenting incidents of workplace violence
- Employee interviews, which include information on any previous incidents of violence
- Actual or potential employee exposure to workplace violence
- Documentation that the workplace violence hazard was reasonably foreseeable by the employer

- Documentation from business groups and associations affiliated with the employer identifying the problem of workplace violence
- Journal articles and research showing the existence of workplace violence in the given industry
- National Institute for Occupational Safety and Health (NIOSH) and OSHA publications related to workplace violence prevention
- National consensus standards
- State and local laws that address workplace violence in specific industries
- Documentation of any employees informing the employer of the hazard or related inspections of the employer
- Employer awareness of any prior incidents, injuries, or close calls related to workplace violence
- Any precautions or protective measures taken by the employer to prevent or minimize workplace violence
- Documentation of how the employer currently addresses workplace violence, including a security plan, training plan, presence of preventative plan, and other safety documents
- Interviews of management, including the person responsible for certifying the OSHA 300 logs
- Employee interviews
- Union complaints
- Employer awareness of local and state laws, that is, state or municipal licensing or accrediting regulations
- Documentation that the workplace violence hazard caused or was likely to cause serious physical harm such as employee interviews, injury and illness logs, and police reports
- Evidence of actual instances where employees were threatened with physical harm or seriously injured or killed as a result of workplace violence
- Documentation of any feasible abatement methods available with an explanation of how they would have materially reduced the hazard

In essence, OSHA is attempting to establish whether the incident was foreseeable, determine if the employer had a violence prevention plan, determine if the plan meet applicable industry standards, and determine if the plan was appropriate considering the criminogenic factors within the locality of the business. If OSHA's determination is unfavorable, the business can expect to be fined and reap the negative publicity after the agency publishes their findings.

OSHA RISK FACTORS

OSHA also lists the following known risk factors to be considered when determining whether to initiate an investigation:

- Working with unstable or volatile persons in certain health-care, social service, or criminal justice setting
- Working alone or in small numbers
- Working late at night or during early morning hours
- Working in high-crime areas
- Guarding valuable property or possessions
- Working in community-based settings, such as community mental health clinics, drug abuse treatment clinics, pharmacies, community-care facilities, and long-term care facilities
- Exchanging money in certain financial institutions
- Delivering passengers, goods, or services
- Having a mobile workplace, such as a taxicab

With this criteria, it is obvious that OSHA's focus is mostly on health-care facilities, correctional facilities, retail and banking operations, and taxi and delivery services, targeting category 1 risks being perpetrated by those with criminal intent and category 2 risks, which is violence committed by a customer, client, or patient. They show few risk factors for acts of violence, harassment, or intimidation committed by a coworker or by an outsider with whom an employee has a personal relationship that has become abusive.

This seems shortsighted because coworker and relationship violence are preeminent factors in workplace-related incidents involving stalking, harassment, and physical assaults. Further, when examining six of the worst workplace violence shootings in the last 15 years – Columbine High School (April 1999, 15 dead and 24 injured); Virginia Tech (April 2007, 33 dead and 23 injured); Aurora, Colorado movie theater (July 2012, 12 dead and 70 injured); Sandy Hook Elementary School (December 2012, 28 dead and 2 injured); Washington Navy Yard (September 2013, 13 dead and 8 injured); and Isla Vista, California (May 2014, 6 dead and 7 injured) – we find that they had nothing in common with the risk factors that OSHA documents in their 2011 directive to their officers. None of these workplaces involved working with unstable or volatile persons, the workplaces were not staffed by one or small numbers of people, they were not businesses with late night or early morning risks, they were not in high-crime areas, the work being done in these locations did not involve guarding valuable property, these were not businesses involved in community-based services, they were not financial institutions, nor were they taxi cabs or delivery services. The facts show that workplace violence can happen anywhere irrespective of surrounding crime rates or whether or not elements in the workplace would be tempting for robbery or other criminal mayhem. To use OSHA's own words "The truth is, workplace violence can strike anywhere, anytime, and no one is immune." [12]

Over the last several years OSHA has evolved and expanded their definition and prioritization of workplace violence issues and it's likely they will continue to do so. While they may not currently be addressing all of the factors we think they should, OSHA has a history of learning and adapting to trends and risks.

OSHA FINES AND LAWSUITS

Should OSHA decide to fine your business, the maximum penalty OSHA can assess, regardless of the circumstances, is $7,000 for each serious violation and $70,000 for a repeated or willful violation. However, there are circumstances whereby OSHA can multiply fines 10-fold. For example,

- If OSHA discovers a violation at your facility and fines you, then later returns and finds that the original violation has not been remediated, you can be fined 10 times the amount of the original fine.
- If OSHA fines you for one violation in a facility and you have multiple facilities within your operation, OSHA can inspect any or all of your additional facilities, and if they find that the same violation is present in one of the other facilities, they can issue you a citation for 10 times the amount of the original fine.
- Additionally, if OSHA fines you because they have determined that an employee was exposed to workplace violence, they can increase that fine by the number of additional employees their investigation shows were also exposed to the same risk. So if an employee files an OSHA complaint because someone who should not have been in your facility assaulted them and OSHA finds that you have no workplace violence prevention plan and determines that your access controls are inadequate, they could fine you $7,000 for the original complaint. If you are a small company with 20 employees, OSHA could also multiply that fine by 20 if they believe that everyone else was also at risk. That fine then becomes $140,000 and could seriously damage the profitability of the company for that fiscal year. If you are a moderate-sized company with 400 employees, there is the potential for OSHA to levy a $2.8 million fine if

they felt that all 400 employees were at risk because of inadequate access controls and lack of a workplace violence prevention plan.

The information just detailed represents potential fines that OSHA could levy in *worst case scenario* situations. It is important to note that OSHA's mission is to improve the safe and healthful work environment within the country, not to drive companies out of business thereby eliminating jobs within the community. The fines are merely tools to incentivize businesses to comply with safety standards and mitigate risks discovered during their investigations. Some recent examples of actual workplace violence–related fines issued by OSHA include:

- $6,300 in fines issued to Danbury Hospital in Danbury, Connecticut, in 2010 after OSHA's investigation revealed 25 cases of injuries to staff members by patients during the prior five years. OSHA found that the hospital's workplace violence plan was incomplete and ineffective at preventing these injuries. [13]
- $8,700 in fines assessed at ResCare Ohio in 2012 for exposing employees to workplace violence at the company's Fairfield, Ohio, resident care facility. OSHA found that employees had been exposed to physical assaults during routine interaction with residents who had a history of violent behavior. [14]
- $78,000 in fines at Brookdale University Hospital and Medical Center in Brooklyn, New York. OSHA found approximately 40 incidents of workplace violence reported between February 7 and April 12, 2014, involving injuries to the head, eye, face, and groin, as well as employees subjected to intimidation and threats during routine interactions with patients and visitors. OSHA found that Brookdale management did not take effective measures to prevent assaults against its employees. OSHA cited Brookdale for one willful violation, with a proposed fine of $70,000, for failing to develop and implement adequate measures to reduce or eliminate the likelihood of physical violence and assaults against employees by patients or visitors. Brookdale was also cited and fined $8,000 for failing to correctly review and certify the OSHA 300A illness and injury reporting form and for not providing forms when requested by the authorized employee representative. [15]
- $71,000 in fines assessed against Corizon Health, a company that provides medical, dental, and psychiatric services to inmates at New York City's Rikers Island Correctional Facility. OSHA's investigation uncovered 39 instances of workplace violence in 2013 involving Corizon employees, up from 8 in 2011. [16]

OHSA is also very serious about protecting employees from retaliation after they have raised concerns to the agency. If OSHA's investigation shows that retaliation was taken against an employee, they will typically file a lawsuit as shown in these examples:

- Helena, Montana (January, 2013) – The U.S. Department of Labor filed a lawsuit in the U.S. District Court for the District of Montana alleging that Helena-based Kbec Inc., a Dairy Queen franchisee, illegally terminated an employee for making complaints regarding workplace violence at the company's facility. [17]
- Fort Lauderdale, Florida (February, 2013) – The U.S. Department of Labor filed a lawsuit in the U.S. District Court for the Middle District of Florida, Fort Myers Division, against Duane Thomas Marine Construction LLC and owner Duane Thomas for terminating an employee who reported workplace violence, in violation of Section 11(c) of the Occupational Safety and Health Act. [18]

WHAT EVERY COMPANY SHOULD DO

1. Have a workplace violence prevention plan:
   a. Communicate what you are doing to prevent violence and disturbing behavior.
   b. Let your employees know what is expected of them.
   c. Let your employees know what to report and how to report it.
2. Make sure your plan is appropriately and actively communicated to all employees so that there is no breakdown of awareness and responsibilities.
3. Review the risks that your company faces (get employee involvement, as employees on the front lines are much more familiar with the risks they face including some that may never have been communicated to management) and take appropriate measures to mitigate those risks.
4. Document your progress and processes.
5. Periodically review incidents and near misses that have occurred to insure that your mitigation plan and processes are still valid and that you have amended your plan and processes to mitigate new risks that have been uncovered. Document and communicate to your employees any and all improvements being made to your workplace violence prevention plan. There will be an in-depth discussion of these topics in Chapter 5.

ENDNOTES

[1] FBI National Incident-Based Reporting System 2012
   http://www.fbi.gov/about-us/cjis/ucr/nibrs/2012

[2] FBI to add "Cruelty to Animals" https://www.osha.gov/workers/index.html to Uniform Crime Report
http://www.fbi.gov/news/podcasts/thisweek/animal-cruelty-category-added-to-nibrs.mp3/view

[3] OSHA definition of workplace violence
https://www.osha.gov/SLTC/workplaceviolence/

[4] FBI crime statistics for 2012
http://www.fbi.gov/about-us/cjis/ucr/nibrs/2012

[5] OSHA statement of nearly 2 million workplace violence victims per year
https://www.osha.gov/SLTC/workplaceviolence/

[6] Robberies not reaching 100,000 in 2011 or 2012
http://www.fbi.gov/about-us/cjis/ucr/nibrs/2011
http://www.fbi.gov/about-us/cjis/ucr/nibrs/2012

[7] Goal of Uniform Crime Report
http://www.fbi.gov/about-us/cjis/ucr/nibrs/2011/resources/about-the-ucr-program

[8] Occupational Safety & Health Administration
https://www.osha.gov/workers/index.html

[9] OSHA General Duty Clause
https://www.osha.gov/pls/oshaweb/owadisp.show_document?p_id=3359&p_table=oshact

[10] OSHA protection for employees against retaliation
https://www.osha.gov/pls/oshaweb/owadisp.show_document?p_table=OSHACT&p_id=3365

[11] OSHA Enforcement Procedures for Investigating or Inspecting Workplace Violence Incidents
https://www.osha.gov/OshDoc/Directive_pdf/CPL_02-01-052.pdf

[12] OSHA statement that workplace violence can strike anywhere
https://www.osha.gov/SLTC/workplaceviolence/

[13] OSHA fine of Danbury Hospital
https://www.osha.gov/pls/oshaweb/owadisp.show_document?p_table=NEWS_RELEASES&p_id=18000

[14] OSHA fine of ResCare
https://www.osha.gov/pls/oshaweb/owadisp.show_document?p_table=NEWS_RELEASES&p_id=23088

[15] OSHA fine of Brookdale University Hospital
https://www.osha.gov/pls/oshaweb/owadisp.show_document?p_table=NEWS_RELEASES&p_id=26514

[16] OSHA fine of Corizon Health
https://www.osha.gov/pls/oshaweb/owadisp.show_document?p_table=NEWS_RELEASES&p_id=26505

[17] OSHA fine of Dairy Queen franchise for retaliation
https://www.osha.gov/as/opa/quicktakes/qt02152013.html ~ 2

[18] OSHA fine of Thomas Marine Construction LLC
https://www.osha.gov/as/opa/quicktakes/qt02152013.html ~ 2

CHAPTER 2

The Need for a Violence Prevention Program

"Management is doing things right; leadership is doing the right things."

—*Peter Drucker*

Contents

Abstract

Many organizations still feel that they do not need a comprehensive workplace violence prevention program. For a wide variety of reasons, they will eschew the notion of spending money and scaring their employees with such a discussion and training. Chapter 2 points out why this is the wrong way to think about having such a program. Besides being the right thing to do, and to ensure that you are preparing your organization to deal with their responsibilities under Occupational Safety and Health Administration (OSHA), there are significant financial losses associated with the aftermath of workplace violence – even for an organization that is prepared. This chapter outlines some of the very real costs and highlights how simple, reasonable preparation can minimize those costs.

Keywords: counseling; crime scene; inappropriate behavior; legal liability; negligent hiring; negligent retention; Occupational Safety and Health Administration (OSHA); protecting employees; trauma; workplace homicide.

In this chapter we explain why your organization should have a violence prevention program. Hopefully the first chapter's emphasis on the Occupational Safety and Health Administration (OSHA) compliance and the fines assessed for not having a violence prevention program will be all the motivation that your organization needs to begin a program of its own.

If not, then let us start with one very succinct and valid reason to institute a violence prevention program: *Protecting your employees is the right thing to do!* To further explain, let us examine the Accent Signage story.

The employees at Accent Signage heard the commotion but couldn't piece together what was happening until the killer was right upon them.

The shooter, 36-year-old employee Andrew Engeldinger, had a history of poor performance and frequent issues of tardiness. According to his family, he also suffered from paranoia and delusions, causing him to become estranged from them as he resisted their attempts to get him into a treatment program.

On September 27, 2012, he was told that he needed to meet with management at 4:30 p.m. to discuss his performance and tardiness issues. A week prior he had received a written reprimand explaining that if his performance did not immediately improve, his employment would be terminated. Engeldinger had a history of clashes with management over his tardiness and performance problems and it had been noted that he was often verbally abrasive with coworkers. He was reminded later in the afternoon of this 4:30 meeting whereupon he went to his car. It is presumed that he knew that the meeting would result in his termination and that his impromptu trip to his car was to retrieve his pistol and a couple of extra loaded magazines.

As soon as he was notified of his termination and handed his final paycheck, he produced his pistol and shot the two men with whom he was meeting. One survived and one didn't. He then shot and killed the company's owner who stepped out of his office to see what was happening. Engeldinger then walked east through a set of double doors, leaving the executive area and entering the sales department. He shot and killed one employee there before moving through another set of double doors that led to the loading area of the business whereupon he shot and killed another employee as well as the UPS driver who was in his truck. From the loading area, he then proceeded through a set of sliding doors and entered the production department. He shot and wounded two employees before heading downstairs to the basement where he took his own life. [1] [2] [3]

Accent Signage is located in the quite Bryn Mawr neighborhood of Minneapolis, where people think that things like this just do not happen in their neighborhood. If you had approached management or the employees of Accent Signage a year earlier and proposed instituting a violence prevention program, they would have most likely told you that things like that don't happen here; yet a heinous act of violence and homicide did happen and unfortunately, they were unprepared.

Management and employees had not been trained to recognize the behavioral warning signs that an employee was struggling and needed help. No one realized that Engeldinger's impromptu trip to his vehicle was a potential danger signal and the lack of lockdown processes ensured that he had free access to roam the various departments allowing him to kill seven people (including himself) and wound two others.

AVOIDANCE OF LEGAL LIABILITY

Along with OSHA compliance and the protection of your employees, another reason to have a viable violence prevention program is to help insulate your company from charges of negligence. Although it is certainly difficult to develop policies and training programs that can anticipate every method and manner by which your company and employees could face an attack, failing to analyze your risks and incorporate reasonable security measures in this day and age is unconscionable and can cause someone to bring a claim against your for one or more of the following:

- Wrongful death, if it can be shown that the death(s) were preventable.
- Negligent practices, if you have no violence prevention plan or if it is found to insufficient.
- Negligent hiring, if you hired someone that you knew or should have known had a history of violence or harassment toward others. If you are not checking prior references and performing background checks then this charge could be brought against you at a later date.
- Negligent retention, if someone who is engaging in violence, harassment, intimidation, or other disruptive behavior is not immediately put on notice that his or her behavior is unacceptable and separated from the company if the inappropriate behavior does not immediately improve.

What Accent Signage's management should have known or did know and what they should have done or failed to do came into question shortly after the incident when a lawsuit was filed by the families of the victims. They charged Accent with negligence as the family's attorney stated that the shootings were "reasonably foreseeable based on Engeldinger's past incidents of employment misconduct and his known propensity for abuse and misconduct."[2] The company's legal team attempted to have the suite dismissed by the court, but on June 2, 2013, a district court judge ruled that the families of the victims could proceed with two negligence counts against Accent Signage because the company did not have policies or training programs for their employees that would mitigate violence nor did they train them on how to survive a violent incident. This ruling was basically aligned with OSHA's guidelines set forth in OSHA's General Duty Clause, which mandates that employers must train their employees on violence prevention and put reasonable safeguards in place.

This ruling squarely puts the blame and legal liability on companies who have done nothing to address the possibility of violent incidents in their workplace. It is clear that violence prevention plans must be addressed in every company's policies and training programs. The lawsuit against Accent was eventually resolved in a confidential settlement arrangement.

THE COST OF AN ON-SITE HOMICIDE

We would like to show you the liability calculations of an approximate cost of a workplace homicide but to do so we need to set some hypothetical parameters. So for this exercise we will use the following assumptions for our conservative estimates:

- Our hypothetical business is a moderately small company employing 200 people who work in two shifts: 125 people work on the first shift and 75 people work on the second shift. The gross revenue for the business is $600,000 per week with a 10% profit margin.
- They have just incurred one employee-to-employee homicide where the shooter, who was an employee, killed one 35-year-old employee (who made $40,000 per year) and then took his own life. The homicide occurred on the first shift during the week between Christmas and the New Year.
- Our hypothetical business has no violence prevention plan.

The first cost that the business will incur after the incident will be *counseling services* for their employees. Because the shooting occurred on the first shift, the entire shift of 125 employees will need to be debriefed and assessed on site by a qualified crisis counseling service:

125 employees × $250 for an on-site assessment = $31,250

We can also assume that some employees from the second shift will experience emotional trauma from the event so we will add another 15 employees who need on-site counseling:

15 employees × $250 for an on-site assessment = $3,750

(Although we are calling it an on-site assessment, it will not actually take place at the business but in conference rooms within nearby hotels.) While many of the employees will not require any further counseling, some certainly will. For this we will assume that 20 people require some on-going counseling, so we will figure those 20 employees will have 12 office visits (rather than on-site counseling) at a rate of $150 per hour amounting to $36,000. Of those 20 employees, perhaps 5 of them will be diagnosed with post-traumatic stress disorder, which could cause $30,000 in ongoing worker's compensation claims for the next year. Once your building reopens, it is a good idea to have two counselors on site for all shifts during the first two days:

2 counselors × 16 hours a day × 2 days = $8,000.

The total first year cost of counseling is $109,000.

The next drain on revenue and profit in the post incident period will be *lost productivity*. Here's what can be expected:

- The building will be closed for crime scene investigation for a minimum of 1.5 days amounting to $150,000 in lost revenue.
- The building will be closed for hazardous waste cleanup and repairs and remodeling. Your employees should not be asked to clean up the blood or the released crime scene area, nor should they be present when this is done. Additionally, bullet holes and other damages should be repaired before the employees return. Assuming that the crime scene was relatively small, we can figure that the business would be closed for an additional two days for another loss in revenue of $200,000.
- Out of respect to the victim and your employees, you will be closed on the day of the employee-victim's funeral for a loss in revenue of $100,000.
- For the first week after the building reopens, you should expect a 25% decline in employee productivity, which would represent a $150,000 decline in revenue.
- **The total loss because of lost productivity would be $600,000.**

Another lost productivity factor is the focus that will be taken off the business in order to prepare for the inevitable lawsuit(s) that will follow. Staff time will be spent retrieving and copying documents for your legal team. Executives and other staff members will spend time being interviewed by your attorneys, being prepped for deposition, and giving their depositions. Even if the suit is settled out of court, significant time will be spent getting to that point.

Next comes the *cost of cleanup, repairs, and remodeling*. As mentioned earlier, your employees should not be involved in these processes. The remaining crime scene will contain blood residue, which is considered hazardous material, therefore a proper hazmat cleanup team will be required. It is important to note that frequently, the shooter does not commit suicide in the same part of the facility where the shooter killed his or her intended target, so you may be dealing with two crime scenes within your building. In addition to the hazmat cleaning of standing blood, carpeted areas drenched with blood will need to be replaced. Blood spatters on chairs, desks, equipment, ceiling walls, and wall coverings will need to be professionally assessed to determine if they can be cleaned or should be replaced. It may also be necessary to remodel the area where the homicides took place. If the victim was shot at his or her cubicle, no one will ever want to be assigned to that space or use that computer again. If the shooting took place in the employee lunchroom, you will need to remodel that portion of the building, build out a new lunchroom, and completely re-do the space where the old lunchroom was. Assuming that no major remodeling is required, you can expect to spend $5,000 to $15,000 on two moderately small crime scene cleanup renovations. For our purposes we will use the middle of the road figure of **$10,000.**

We are now at the point where it is prudent to consider the *cost of the lawsuit*. Most lawsuits related to workplace violence are settled out of court and as such, the ultimate costs to the employer are not revealed. However, on December 3, 1993, $4.25 million was awarded to a postal employee shot by a coworker in Dearborn, Michigan. The award is higher than those of which we are aware and the fact that the employee was *awarded* this money is an indication that an out-of-court settlement could not be reached and the case went to court.

A good place to start in our model is to figure the salary that the victim would have earned had he worked through age 65. As we mentioned in our hypothetical assumptions, our victim was 35 years of age making $40,000 per year. Therefore, assuming he would have worked another 30 years at the same wage, the lost income to his survivors would be $1.2 million with approximately $500,000 spent in legal services for a total lawsuit cost of $1.7 million.

The plaintiff's counsel will always ask for more damages for such things as emotional distress, cost of counseling for his or her family, and so forth. Additionally the family may be able to negotiate or be awarded more money if they can make the case that the business was particularly negligent. Two of the most common factors that can be used to increase the settlement or award are (1) the lack of a violence prevention plan and (2) foreseeability, meaning that the business knew or should have known that the aggressor's behavior would ultimately escalate into an act of violence.

For our purposes, we will assume that these additional factors were dropped as part of the out-of-court negotiation and that your company's total damages and cost remain at **$1.7 million**. However if more than one employee was killed or seriously injured, you could expect a significantly higher settlement. There may also be lawsuits from employees who feel that you needlessly exposed them to danger because of a lack of preparedness.

The next cost to the business will be turnover. Not all of your employees are going to come back to work. The combined cost of recruiting and training a new employee in nontechnical businesses is considered to be approximately $2500. If the person is in information technology, an executive, or a licensed professional (doctor or pharmacist), the cost of replacement may rise beyond $25,000. For our example, we will assume that 10% of the employees (20 people total) do not want to return. We will further assume that 15 of them are staff members and 5 of them are executives. Their cost of replacement will be **$155,000.**

At this point, the total cost of the one-workplace homicide/suicide is **$2,574,000.** As bad as this number is, there are still other incremental costs that could be looming, much to the detriment of your business. These are basically business partners that are unsure about continuing to do business with you unless you are a very large resilient company.

- Vendors may be concerned about your company's future stability and decline to extend credit or may discontinue their relationship altogether until they can determine your financial future.
- Clients may be concerned about your company's stability and abandon you for a competitor.
- Shareholders may feel that your short-term investment value is bleak and sell.
- New clients may be reluctant to want to do business with your company.
- Banks may be reluctant to extend any further loans.
- There may be insurance and health-care increases coming your way.

Now let's see how the cost of the violent incident affected the company's profitability. The yearly projected profit for the year (10% of $600,000/ week × 52 weeks) is $3,120,000. The total incident cost of $2,574,000 negates 83% of our model company's profit for the year.

As we conclude this chapter, we hope you realize that, as we mentioned earlier, we took a very conservative approach in looking at the costs of having an on-site homicide and suicide. Depending on the size of your company and the other factors just mentioned, your costs could be somewhat below the $2,574,000 provided by our model or they could be significantly higher. An interesting exercise that we recommend would be to use our model and plug in the numbers that would be applicable to your business. Between what we have provided you in Chapters 1 and 2, you should have enough information to convince any function in your company that you need a violence prevention plan.

ENDNOTES

[1] Police reports detail witness accounts of Accent Signage shooting http://www.myfox-twincities.com/story/19751294/accent-signage-police-reports-detail- witness-accounts

[2] In Minneapolis Accent Signage shooting suit, settlement reached http://www.twincities.com/localnews/ci_26583554/minneapolis-accent-signage-shooting-suit-settlement-reached

[3] Accent Signage shooting victim's family sues Minneapolis company http://www.twincities.com/ci_22498303/minneapolis-family-accent-signage-shooting-victim-sues

CHAPTER 3

Overcoming Rationalizations, Objections, and Denials

"Men often oppose a thing merely because they have had no agency in planning it, or because it may have been planned by those whom they dislike."
—Alexander Hamilton

Contents

Abstract

Chapter 3 examines what may be the biggest obstacle to the creation of a comprehensive workplace violence prevention program, which is the tendency of senior management to fall victim to various common rationalizations, objections, and denials (RODs). A commonly stated reason for not pursuing such a program is the fear that employees will be frightened by the mere discussion of the subject. Other arguments range from the costs involved to the organization's facilities being located in a relatively low-crime area. In short, many arguments can be, and often are, made that shut down the discussion before it begins. Overcoming such arguments requires a calm response that breaks down each argument with facts – not emotions or half-truths. Historical data, a thorough understanding of the requirements and expectations under Occupational Safety and Health Administration (OSHA), and the realization that few well-positioned leaders like having a program such as this developed or conceived by anyone else, can help make the discussion easier and result in gaining acceptance and approval.

Keywords: imminent danger; Occupational Safety and Health Administration (OSHA); rationalizations, objections, denials (RODs); training; violence prevention

Sheila had had enough. She started her car on that warm spring evening, turned on the headlights, and then opened her garage door, whereupon she saw that the strange car and the silhouette of the male occupant in her driveway again. The strange car's headlights turned on and it quickly reversed out of her driveway and sped away. Sheila was sure she knew who it was and she was determined that this should finally come to an end. She pulled out behind the car, called the police, and read the license plate number to the dispatcher as she followed him along local roads.

Soon red and blue flashing lights filled Sheila's rearview mirror as units of the sheriff's department caught up with them and pulled the suspect vehicle to the side of the road. In very short order Shelia's suspicions were confirmed as the driver who was parked in her driveway was identified as Adrian, a coworker. Shelia explained to the officers that Adrian had been stalking her for several years. She declined to press charges against him but did request that a report be filed so that she could take a copy to her manager at work as well as have one on hand should she decide to obtain a restraining order.

On the following day Sheila met with her manager, gave him a copy of the report, and firmly requested that more definitive action be taken than occurred the last time that she reported Adrian's unwanted attention and actions. Her manager notified the human resource manager who requested that the security department conduct a thorough investigation.

The security department met with Sheila right away and ascertained the following facts. Adrian worked in the same department with Shelia but they initially had no social contact inside or outside of the workplace. Adrian was a loner and Sheila was a single parent with several children.

After Sheila's marriage ended, Adrian began inquiring his coworkers to see if they thought Shelia liked him. Soon Sheila noted changes in Adrian's behavior. Although he limited his conversations with her, discussing only departmental business, he was always around. He hovered around her workstation and eavesdropped on her conversations and phone calls. Coworkers soon noted that he would come in early to rifle through her desk. His behavior escalated as he used the information gleaned from her day planner to stalk her outside of the workplace. He seemed to casually turn up everywhere she went.

Soon Shelia met with her manager and gave a detailed reporting of Adrian's unwanted attention and actions. At this point the manager attempted to handle the situation himself. Their organization did not have strong policies related to stalking and harassment of a coworker and the manager merely met with Adrian who denied all accusations and no further action was taken. No thorough investigation was conducted; no coworkers were interviewed to ascertain what they had observed and overheard, and thus there was no change in Adrian's behavior.

This time, however, now that the company had a firm policy on stalking and harassment and the security department, human resources, and the legal department were involved, a thorough investigation was conducted. After interviewing and taking statements from Sheila and coworker witnesses, the security representatives confronted Adrian with evidence that he could not refute. Adrian admitted to being obsessed with Sheila and admitted to every allegation made against him. The decision was made to give Adrian one more chance and transfer him to another nearby location. While Adrian admitted to being obsessed with Sheila, he had no history of violence nor was he assessed to have any inclination toward violence at the present time. Therefore Adrian's access to the building Shelia worked in was terminated and he was admonished never to return to her work location. This decision was communicated to him on a Friday. Early Monday morning coworkers found him again rifling through Sheila's workspace. Security was summoned and found that Adrian had piggybacked in when another employee used her access card to enter an unmonitored side entrance. This time Adrian was terminated.

The fact that this organization previously had no firm policy on stalking or harassment and how allegations of such should be handled put them at a huge liability risk because the first time Sheila reported his unwanted behavior, it was inappropriately handled and she continued to be victimized for several additional years.

Not having a comprehensive program for violence prevention, which defines all facets of inappropriate behavior (including stalking, harassment, and all other elements found in the Occupational Safety and Health Administration [OSHA] definition of violence) is inconceivable. The subject matter, however, makes some decision makers uncomfortable and when presenting a violence prevention proposal, it is not uncommon for it to be met with pushback, usually stated in the form of a rationalization, an objection, or a denial (more simply referred to as a *ROD*). The most common RODs thrown against violence prevention programs are the following:

- We can't train our people.
- Our employees won't listen, comprehend, or remember it.
- How often does this really happen?

- We don't need this because our employees are one big happy family.
- The training will upset our employees.
- We don't want to give anyone any ideas.
- We have a guard at the front desk; we should be okay.

- It's not in the budget.
- We can't afford to take the employees away from their workstation for a one-hour training session.
- We've never had any reports of trouble in the past, so why do we suddenly need this?

- We don't need this because our facility is in a very low crime area.

- This training will send the message that we think there is imminent danger.
- We have someone (or some department) who already handles this.
- This training will prompt people to make frivolous allegations.

Each of the preceding 14 RODs fall into one of three categories:

1. **Financial** RODs
2. **Operational** RODs
3. RODs based on a **lack of subject matter expertise**
   Let's tackle these categories one at a time.

Financial RODs

It's not in the budget!   This probably a true statement, but if you accept "no" for an answer, your program will never get wings.

Financial RODs

	In facing this ROD, it is important to have someone from the finance department as a part of your group. Just because you or your department does not have the budget doesn't mean that the money is not in the organization somewhere. There may be another group that has postponed a major project and therefore has a budget surplus for the year. You don't have line of sight into other departments' budget performance but the finance department does, and this is invaluable knowledge.
	Even if the organization does not have one department with a large surplus, your finance representative might be able to find 10 departments who could each relinquish 10% of their budget.
	As a last resort ask how much of a budget you can be given. If the organization can only spare $1,000, you can get your plan proposed, approved, and start an informational poster program. This will make the workplace a little bit safer and show that you have a program that has been approved, an implementation schedule, and demonstrated that you have made progress.
We can't afford to take our employees away from their workstations for a one-hour training session.	Then bring the training to them! Another key ally to have on your team is a representative from your organization's training department. Work with them to parse out the training in smaller bites that do not disrupt the normal work processes.
	• Add a 10-minute violence prevention topic to weekly departmental meetings.
	• Produce a 15-minute weekly training module that employees can complete online at their workstation. In four weeks your one-hour training session has been accomplished!

Operational RODs

We can't train our employees. Our employees won't listen, comprehend, or remember it.	These two rationalizations are troubling as they are condescending and insulting to your employees. All employees working in your organization have been trained to do their jobs. Employees like useful, meaningful training and everyone cares about their workplace safety. Your employees have seen news reports regarding workplace violence and their children are practicing lockdown drills in school. This topic is very much on their minds.

(Continued)

Lack of Subject Matter Expertise

How often does this really happen?	According to OSHA this happens about 2 million times a year in varying formats from harassment to homicide (see the OSHA definition of workplace violence discussed in Chapter 1).
We've never had any reports of trouble in the past.	This rationalization usually comes from an organization where there is no vehicle for reporting incidents or where the incident reports are not shared with the decision maker making this statement. It is a good idea to have a response for this statement before it is made. If there are reported incidents, know how many and whether they were threats, disturbing behavior, harassment, physical assault, etc. If there is no vehicle for reporting incidents within the organization be prepared to speak to that as well. If you have not told employees that they must report incidents as defined in OSHA's definition of workplace violence and if you have not provided a vehicle whereby those incidents can be reported, then you are not in compliance with OSHA and you are negligent for not knowing what may be occurring within your organization. Finally, it has been our experience with our clients that after receiving the violence prevention training 2% of your organization's population will come forward and report that they have a restraining order against an outside third party who is harassing, stalking, abusing, or assaulting them. If your workforce contains a mere 500 people, then this is 10 potential acts of violence that could occur on your premises that, heretofore, you knew nothing about.
We don't need this because our employees are one big happy family.	This is a statement of naïve denial usually made by someone who is near the top of the ivory tower and has no idea what is going on in the lower levels of the organization. Further, as will be discussed in the next chapter, the number one cause of workplace incidents are related to relationship violence. This is violence caused by someone not related to your workplace who commits the violent act on your premises against one of your employees. So even if your employees are one big happy family, do their outside relationships maintain the same stability?

Lack of Subject Matter Expertise

We don't need this because our facility is in a low crime area.	Surrounding crime statistics are not a factor in predicting the likelihood of workplace-related violence. Area crime statistics are great if you are analyzing your security needs to prevent robbery, burglary, auto theft, etc., but they play no role in predicting workplace violence. Workplace violence is an interpersonal crime that crosses all demographics and socioeconomic factors. Facilities in a low-crime area may even be at a greater risk because they typically lack the security precautions taken in facilities that reside in a higher crime area. Facilities in high-crime area usually have security guards, a fenced-in and controlled parking lot, good lighting, closed circuit TV systems covering the premises, and some form of access control on the facility and on the interior departments. Facilities in lower risk areas usually do not have the same semblance of security.
The training will upset our employees.	Lt. Col. David Grossman, author of the Pulitzer Prize nominated book *On Killing*, discussed this rationalization in his seminar "The Bulletproof Mind." Grossman explained that this rationalization was used when fire drills were being introduced into school systems in the late 1950s. People pushed back on fire marshals thinking that children would have nightmares about fires if they participated in fire drills. [1] As everyone knows, this did not happen. Your employee's children are now participating in lockdown drills and your employees are wondering why you aren't doing them as well.
This will send a message that we think there is imminent danger.	It could, depending on how the message is constructed. The correct message is that the organization "is being proactive and in light of the many incidents that we see in the news media, we are instituting a program to help us prevent violence from occurring in our organization."
We don't want to give anyone any ideas.	There is absolutely no data to suggest that violence prevention training causes violence. If anything, it may bring attention to situations that are already percolating within the workplace and need to be corrected. If there is someone in your organization with the predilection toward violence, this training and associated programs will not escalate his or her behavior.

(Continued)

Lack of Subject Matter Expertise

We already have someone or some group that handles this.	What is the person's or group's level of training and experience? Are they trained in conducting and documenting investigations? Are they trained to assess behaviors and actions and build effective plans to safely manage these incidents or are their responses purely emotional and steeped in disciplinary action as the be-all and end-all solution? If the answers to these questions show a lack of depth in the training and experience of these people, then the status quo of your organization's readiness needs to be reviewed.
We have a security guard at the front desk; we should be fine.	What is the level of training and experience of the guard? Is the guard armed? And if so, what is the level of training? Most guards are responsible to observe, report, and handle visitor administration. If an estranged husband entered the facility with a shotgun to kill his wife, is your guard trained to handle that incident or would your guard merely be the first victim. To look at it another way, if a fire was started in your lobby, you have fire extinguishers and your guard is trained in how to use them to extinguish the fire before it becomes deadly. The guard has the training and tools to handle a fire; does the guard have the training and tools to handle the shotgun-wielding ex-husband?
This training will prompt people to make false or frivolous allegations.	This has certainly not been our experience. Everyone takes a violence prevention program very seriously. There are issues going on within your organization at this very moment that you don't know about. It is always best to find out about them when they are smaller issues that are easier to handle than to find out about them after a violent incident has occurred.

Although we have dealt with the most common RODs, it is also important to understand that the RODs themselves may not be the full reason the individual who uttered them is opposing you. The RODs that the person stated might just be smoke to cover up real concerns. In most of these instances, the person or group does not want to vocalize real concerns because their concerns may tend to make them look insensitive or selfish.

The most common concerns we have encountered are:

- The person or group just doesn't think that violence prevention planning and training are necessary.
- They think you are impeding upon territory they own.

- They think that your proposal is going to add work to their plate, which is already overloaded.
- They don't want to hear this message from you.

The goal is to turn their concern into an advantage for you. Let's deal with these one at a time.

The Planning and Training Aren't Necessary

Although someone might actually feel this way, you have been provided a lot of factual reasons to overcome this obstacle. The truth is that sadly, violence occurring in the workplace has become a more common method for individuals to air their real or perceived grievances. Whether the attacker feels justified in taking revenge for some perceived slight that occurred on the job; whether the attacker has determined that if he or she can't have the object (person) of obsession, who happens to be your employee, then no one can; or whether the attacker feels that a public mass homicide is a warranted means of fulfilling an ideology with which he or she has become aligned, these attacks are occurring with greater frequency and resulting in higher death tolls.

Because of this, OSHA requires that your organization have a plan and that it be effective. That fact, and that fact alone, should be reason enough to ultimately win your case for a violence prevention program.

Your Proposal Is Encroaching into Someone Else's Territory

Another reason that others might push back on your proposal is because they feel that this subject falls into their job description or their department's realm. They may feel that they already have the bases covered even though they do not have a documented and socialized plan. Unfortunately this individual doesn't understand that a comprehensive and effective plan requires a multidisciplinary team to develop policies, processes, and training and bring about the changes needed in the workplace.

As soon as you identify the person or group, meet with that person or group and win them over. Lay out your facts in a cogent manner so that the person or group pushing back agree with your facts. Sometimes you can even get them to make your proposal for you and purport that is their idea. If so, this is a win–win all the way around!

Your Proposal Will Add Work to Their Plate

This is a common concern that can result in a ROD. The best way to combat this concern is to meet it head on. When you make your proposal, state that you and your team will bear the major workload and that the participation of the other groups will be small, mainly in the role of advisor or approver to the work your group is doing. Prior to your proposal meeting, you may want to socialize this with some of the individuals who will hear your proposal and relieve them of this concern before your formal proposal meeting.

They Don't Want to Hear This Message from You

This is a tough one, but it does happen: For whatever reason, they just don't want to hear this message from you. We have worked with organizations that did not want the proposal to be given by someone on their staff; they wanted the presentation to be given by someone from our consulting group. Similarly, other clients wanted to hear the proposal from their own people, not the paid consultants. In other instances, we have seen well-prepared and delivered proposals get stymied simply because the person presenting the proposal was of a lower rank than everyone else at the table.

Ways to combat this are to make sure that your proposal program is aligned with your organization's core values, mission statement, and other programs that are currently important within your company. For example, one client made employee wellness one of their core values. They provided good medical benefits, put a gym in their facility, hired a trainer to provide off-the-clock workout sessions, and offered incentives for the employees to lose weight and quit smoking. Violence prevention became a natural outreach of their overall wellness program.

Another valuable approach is to have an executive sponsor who believes in your proposed program and can assist your efforts by getting you in front of the people you with whom you need to talk. The executive sponsor lends legitimacy to your program and your executive sponsor also has the CEO's ear. Nothing takes the roadblocks down faster than if the CEO announces that your program is an organizational priority.

ENDNOTE

[1] Lt. Col. David Grossman, "The Bulletproof Mind" (presentation, Eden Prairie, MN, November 9, 2013).

PART II

Getting Everyone Up-to-Speed

CHAPTER 4

Types of Violence

"If you take out the killings, Washington actually has a very, very low crime rate."
—Marion Barry, former mayor of Washington, D.C.

Abstract

The generic term, *workplace violence*, has been broken down into four universally accepted categories: criminal intent, customer/patient/client, coworker, and personal relationship. This is as defined by the Occupational Safety and Health Administration (OSHA) and is also called out by the Federal Bureau of Investigation (FBI) in their writings on the topic. The authors prefer to break this down into three main areas: external violence, associate violence, and personal-relationship violence, which is statistically the most commonly reported type. Common misconceptions of the subject of workplace violence include the myth, perpetuated by the media, that rampage shooters pose a growing and continuous threat to society. In fact, far greater numbers of homicides occur within intimate interpersonal relationships. This violence often spills over into the workplace.

Keywords: active shooters; associate violence; criminal intent; Dylann Roof; external violence; Occupational Safety and Health Administration (OSHA); personal relationship violence

As mentioned earlier, getting accurate statistics regarding workplace violence is a slippery slope. Federal and local law enforcement do not have a standard definition of workplace-related violence and do not make any attempt to break it out. The Occupational Safety and Health Administration (OSHA) makes an attempt at providing definitions with their four types of workplace violence:

Type 1 is *criminal intent*—violent acts by people who enter the workplace to commit a robbery or other crime, or current or former employees who enter the workplace with the intent to commit a crime.

Type 2 is *customer/client/patient*—violence directed at employees by customers clients, patients, students, inmates, or any other to whom the employee provides a service.

Type 3 is *coworker*—violence directed at a coworker, supervisor, or manager by a current or former employee, supervisor, or manager.

Type 4 is *personal*—violence in the workplace by someone who does not work there but who is known to, or has a personal relationship with, an employee. [1]

Although the OSHA model has its merits, we do not like to use it as a model for most businesses and other organizations. Specifically, we do not like to include criminal intent in our model as, in most (but not all) cases, the criminal came into the business to commit a property crime, such as a robbery or other type of theft, and violence only ensued after an employee attempted to intervene or did not cooperate with the robbery. Most companies where these types of crimes take place have preventive measures and security hardware in place to prevent the crime and policies that prohibit the employees from attempting to intervene in matters for which they are neither trained nor equipped. We certainly feel that data related to robberies, burglaries, thefts, and other business-related crime where violence might take place should be collected, analyzed, and reported, but we feel that their inclusion in workplace violence data skews the results and takes the focus away from incidents where violence was committed solely for the sake of an attack on others.

For our clients, we prefer to classify workplace violence as emanating from three source types:

1. External violence is violence perpetrated by individuals who are unknown to the organization. This would include the *active shooter*, who we prefer to refer to as the *rampage shooter*.

2. Associate violence is a broader term we use to include employees, students, clients, members of a house of worship, and so forth. As the name

implies, this is violence that is perpetrated by those who are associated with the organization.

3. Personal-relationship violence is violence that is perpetrated by someone who is or was in a real or (in many cases) perceived romantic relationship with the victim.

Now you might very well be thinking that category 3, personal-relationship violence, could easily be included in the other two categories. If the victim's relationship with the perpetrator was outside the organization, it would fall into the external violence category and if the relationship was with someone else in the business, it would fall into the associate violence category. This is certainly a valid point. We chose to make personal-relationship violence its own category as it is the most frequent type of risk that your organization will encounter. This might come as a surprise to some readers because it is the rampage shooters who get the media coverage while the woman who is killed by her ex-boyfriend does not get the same attention in national headlines.

Active shooting incidents gain national attention because of the number of people killed in one location at one time. For example, on June 17, 2015, Dylann Roof allegedly killed nine parishioners at the Mother Emanuel African Methodist Episcopal (A.M.E.) Church in Charleston, South Carolina. Even six days after the incident, the tragic shooting was still a top news story.

Although active shooters, such as the one in Charleston, are certainly worthy of the media attention they derive, the actual numbers pale in comparison to the number of relationship violence deaths that occur each year. A report by the Federal Bureau of Investigation (FBI) of active shooting incidents between 2000 and 2013 shows that there were 11.4 active shootings per year with about 3 people killed per incident or 34 killed per year. [2] According to the Centers for Disease Control and Prevention (CDC), 1300 women die each year at the hands of an intimate partner. [3] Further, the CDC estimates that 1.3 million women per year are the victims of a physical assault by an intimate partner. The American Medical Association (AMA) reports that one in three women will be assaulted by a domestic partner in their lifetimes. [4] The AMA estimates that the yearly number of victims could be as high as 4 million in any given year.

Although active shooter incidents are certainly horrific in nature, it is clearly time that our nation realize that relationship violence is a huge societal problem and put the appropriate resources in victim treatment and preventive measures.

Please note that we recognize that both men and women can be the aggressors in relationship abuse. Reported cases, however, predominately show men as the aggressors and females as the victims. According to the Bureau of Justice Statistics, 85% of domestic violence victims are women. [4] Therefore we tend to refer to the aggressors as "he" and victims as "she" in our discussion of the observable symptoms of relationship abuse.

ENDNOTES

[1] OSHA Instruction: Enforcement Procedures for Investigating or Inspecting Workplace Violence Incidents, Directive CPL 02-01-052, September 8, 2011
https://www.osha.gov/OshDoc/Directive_pdf/CPL_02-01-052.pdf
[2] A Study of Active Shooter Incidents in the United States between 2000 and 2013, Federal Bureau of Investigation, U.S. Department of Justice
https://www.fbi.gov/news/stories/2014/september/fbi-releases-study-on-active-shooter-incidents/pdfs/a-study-of-active-shooter-incidents-in-the-u.s.-between-2000-and-2013
[3] Costs of Intimate Partner Violence against Women in the United States, National Center for Injury Prevention and Control, Centers for Disease Control and Prevention, Department of Health and Human Services
http://www.cdc.gov/violenceprevention/pdf/IPVBook-a.pdf
[4] Fast Facts on Domestic Violence, the Clark County Prosecuting Attorney
http://www.clarkprosecutor.org/html/domviol/facts.htm

Relationship Violence

"My father was one of those men who sit in a room and you can feel it: the simmer, the sense of some unpredictable force that might, at any moment, break loose, and do something terrible."
—*John Burnside*, A Lie About My Father: A Memoir

Contents

Abstract

Chapter 5 examines relationship violence. Relationship violence is perhaps the most pervasive social issue of our day, and it is often the most underreported. Police in every jurisdiction, regardless of socioeconomic, educational, religious, or other standing, commonly deal with the issue of violence between intimates. In many of these cases, the violence, or threat of violence, is not reported until it becomes tragic. In other cases, one party will report the ongoing issues to the police, but not to his or her employer. Many victims of relationship violence are afraid to let their employers know for fear of losing their jobs. This reality can result in serious repercussions for organizations, which can be caught flat-footed when the domestic violence spills over into the workplace. Organizations need to take simple, yet profoundly impactful, steps to ensure they are aware when an employee is a victim of such abuse. Taking proactive steps such as training employees in what to look for, and how to safely and discreetly report their concerns or suspicions, is a reasonable and smart way to help prevent tragedy.

Keywords: abuse; domestic violence; Employee Assistance Program (EAP); human degradation; relationship violence

The prominence of relationship violence in our modern society is a social blight akin to the terrible human degradation brought by slavery in our country's early existence.

Ben worked the second shift, which meant he would normally get home between 12:30 and 1 a.m. When he walked in the door at 8:20 p.m., everyone in the family knew that something must have happened at work, but no one wanted to ask. He poured himself bourbon on the rocks and settled into his reclining chair in the living room where his wife, Joan, and his 16-year-old son James were watching TV. Joan was putting together a binder of material for the real estate licensing course she was about to begin. Although he feigned approval of this enterprise when he was sober, he ultimately despised Joan's venture. As with most wife abusers, he maintained control over her by making her feel worthless and by making her financially dependent on his income. While Joan continued assembling the binder, Ben sat there glaring at Joan with contempt. James noticed this and prayed that his mother would just put the binder and the real estate materials away. She continued, and James watched as his father's already abhorrent mood escalated.

At about 10 p.m., Joan competed the binder and took it into the kitchen and set it on the counter by the door to the garage. Ben soon followed her and James could tell by the speed and tenacity with which he exited the recliner that the evening was going to go from bad to worse. He could hear his father making vile comments to Joan in a low guttural voice. Within seconds the sounds of a scuffle erupted, and James rounded the corner to see his father strangling his mother. He grabbed his father's shoulders and was attempting to get in between his parents when his older sister, Rona, came bounding down the stairs yelling, "Stop it, stop it, please stop it." Ben disengaged, and Rona took Joan upstairs where she would spend the night in Rona's bedroom.

James realized that his father needed to be distracted and deescalated, otherwise round two would soon begin and it would be worse than round one. James asked his father to sit down, hoping to engage him in a little kitchen-table diplomacy. James interwove a lot of topics into the conversation and after a little more than an hour, he came around to the subject of how his father's violent episodes were destroying Ben's relationship with his wife and family. Eventually Ben took James's hand and apologized. Ben then began to tell James how much he loved him. This went on for another hour until James pointed out how late it was, and as he had school the next day, he needed to get to sleep. Ben agreed and as they both stood up, Ben asked his son for a hug. Thinking that they had made progress during this talk, James went forward and hugged his father. That is when Ben attempted to sexually assault James. James pushed Ben away, whereupon Ben made another attempt. James pushed him away again and told Ben that his actions were inappropriate. At that point they made their way upstairs where Ben tried to entice James to come into his bedroom. James declined. A few minutes later Ben entered James's room, sat down on the bed and once again, this time a little more sternly, tried to demand he come into his room. James again rebuffed Ben's advances and wondered if he could roll off the other side of his bed and get to the old and dull World War II bayonet that he had recently purchased and kept under the bed. Fortunately, his father left and went back into his own bedroom.

The next day Rona left the house and went to stay with a friend. James was tired and distraught but preferred to be a sleepy student than stay at home. James did, however, miss his after-school shift at his part-time job. Joan missed her shift at the bank in which she worked and her subsequent first day of real estate school as she was upset, fatigued, and didn't want anyone to see the bruises on her neck. (Relationship abuse is a very personal form of violence as it is meant to demonstrate the power and control the abuser has over his or her victim. Abusers tend to use their hands much more often than a weapon. School districts across the country would be doing the women of this nation a great service if physical education classes for female students focused on self-defense and self-esteem empowerment. Helping young women to become competent in breaking chokeholds and wrist grabs and teaching groin strikes, coupled with abuse awareness and social resources, would be a wonderful additional to the physical education curriculum.)

The family never spoke of this episode again.

There is no doubt that the abuse outlined in the preceding case is horrific, but the question that arises from it is whether this situation is of any concern to the businesses where Joan and Ben are employed. The family is in crisis, they are embarrassed, they think they are the only ones going through this traumatic stress, and they don't know where to turn for help. But nothing involved in this incident took place on company premises, so it does not touch the business – right? No, it definitely does have a major effect on the business even though the abuse is taking place at home.

First let's look at the scope and consequences of relationship abuse. In adults, about 1 out of every 4 women and 1.5 out of every 10 men are victimized in an abusive relationship. Along with the physical injuries that are associated with the abuse, the victims are also more likely to contract chronic diseases that may plague them for the rest of their life. Abused women are 70% more likely to develop heart disease, 80% more likely to experience a stroke, and 60% more likely to develop asthma than women who are not in abusive relationships.

So the first relationship violence area of impact is health care. If your organization provides medical benefits to your employees, relationship abuse is driving up your costs by increases in medical care, paid medical days off, and lost productivity to the tune of $8 billion a year in the United States. This constitutes $5.8 billion in medical costs and $2.5 billion in lost productivity. The $6 billion in increased medical costs means that employers pay more for their health-care benefit programs, and some increases in coverage and deductible costs are passed along to the employee base. Identifying and intervening in relationship abuse before it becomes a medical issue can help curb your health-care costs. [1] [2] [3] [4] [5] Rising health-care costs affect everyone. Remember, relationship violence is directly affecting 24% of your female employees and 14% of your male associates. It also indirectly affects many of your other staff members as well. When your victimized employees lose workdays because of their injuries, fatigue, and depression, other employees have to pick up the slack. This can cause a drain in employee wellness and morale. An employee victimized by relationship violence can also cause a security risk for your other employees as demonstrated in the next case study.

Week 1: The call came in to the corporate security director late on a Friday afternoon. Ray, the manager of an organization in a small town, called to report that last week he had, once again, suspended an employee named Diane because of unexcused absences. The current absence was her final warning as prescribed by the organization's policies and she had been suspended for one week. Ray stated that he had just called Diane to inform her of her schedule for the upcoming week, whereupon her husband, Jim, answered the phone. Jim told Ray that if he didn't stop "fucking with his wife," he would kill Ray. Ray related that he didn't really think Jim would kill him, but he wanted to know if he could fire Diane over the threats made by her husband. A subsequent discussion with the human resources and employee relations department determined that they would not terminate Diane over her husband's threat. The security director, knowing that unexcused absences are frequently a symptom of domestic violence, asked Ray if he had any reason to believe that Diane was in an abusive relationship. Ray did not think so. The security director then asked if Diane had ever shown up for work with visible signs of bruising or shown evidence of trying to cover up bruising. After a few moments of thought, Ray did remember a time when Diane wore long-sleeved blouses during an uncomfortable heat wave. Toward the end of the week, she came in wearing short sleeves, but many employees noted that she had applied makeup on her arms to cover up bruises. He also remembered another instance where she wore sunglasses for a week. Ray and many others commented to themselves that when they looked at Diane from the side, it was evident that she had two black eyes.

At this point there was no direct threat toward anyone in the facility and no actual evidence to support the assumption that Diane was being abused at home. The organization felt the need to do something but needed to be cautious at this juncture. They decided to have Ray meet with Diane on her return to work and provide her with a clear but tactful message.

First, Ray explained the seriousness of the absence policy and made sure Diane fully understood that her next unexcused absence would result in her termination. It was hoped that she would go home and reiterate that information to her husband Jim so that they were both aware that the next absence would result in her separation from the company. In this way Jim would not be surprised if Diane lost her job.

Second, Ray explained to Diane that there may be many reasons why someone may have difficulty making it to work and the company had an employee assistance plan whose counselors were adept at helping people resolve whatever issue affected their attendance reliability. Ray then gave her a business card for the employee assistance plan and even offered to dial the phone number for her and leave the room. Diane politely declined the offer for assistance and went back to work.

Week 5: For several weeks nothing further happened. On day 28 after Diane's return to work, Ray called the security director late on a Friday afternoon. He stated that on the previous Monday, Diane came to work with obvious evidence that she had been assaulted. Diane explained that on Sunday evening, Jim had become enraged because she had not put a tool back in its proper place. He pushed her through the door leading into the garage, threw her to the garage floor, and began beating her about the head and shoulders. During the attack, her adult daughter walked in, as she was supposed to be going to dinner with them. She told Jim to stop his assault and told him she was calling the police. He responded, "Go ahead and call them, I'll kill them all." On the arrival of the police, Diane was taken to the hospital to have her injuries examined, while Jim was booked into the city jail for assault.

Diane then told Ray that she was going to stay with a friend who lived in another state to get away from Jim for an undetermined amount of time. She was leaving right away so that she could get out before Ray had his bond hearing and came home.

Ray told Diane that Jim had been calling the company everyday asking to speak to Diane. Jim was continually told that Diane was not there. Finally, Jim told the receptionist who took his call to tell Diane that if she pursued the criminal charges against him, he would kill her. He further told the receptionist that if he could not get to Diane, then he would come to the company's facility and get Ray. He went on to say that if he could not get to Ray, he would get Ray's wife and then recited Ray's home address to the receptionist to show that he was serious. The receptionist then relayed the message to Ray and many other employees within the organization. Several of the women in the facility told Ray that they had told their husbands of Ray's call and several of the husbands were going to sit in the parking lot with their shotguns in case Jim showed up. Ray did not have any phone numbers for where Diane would be staying, so there was no way to follow up with her and get more information about Jim.

The security director dispatched an investigator to visit the police department with two purposes: Arrange off-duty police coverage for Ray's facility and find out what they knew about Ray. On meeting with the watch commander, the investigator learned that just about every officer on the police force had experienced a run-in with Jim. The watch commander explained that several years ago, Jim had been involved in a serious industrial accident at his place of employment. Since then he had exhibited violent and paranoid tendencies. The watch commander stated that Jim had gotten in several physical altercations because he thought that he was being followed. He approached cars at stoplights or forced them over to the side of the road and assaulted the drivers who he perceived to be following him. In the past this also included assaults to police officers who may have been behind him in traffic. The watch commander suggested that the company take Jim's threats seriously.

Off-duty police officers were hired to safeguard the facility and manager; supervisors and receptionists were instructed that if Jim called he was to be politely informed that as the company did not know where Diane was or when she would be returning, they would be unable to take any messages for her from him. Ray reported that over the next two weeks, Jim's calls became less frequent and his demeanor was less intimidating.

Week 7: Two weeks later Diane returned to work and told Ray that she was going to be staying with her daughter for the time being. The security investigator interviewed Diane, and her statements confirmed what the watch commander had relayed to the investigator. Diane further related that Jim was keeping a baseball bat along the driver's seat in his car. She also stated that he had several firearms and frequently kept one in his vehicle as well. The company determined that her presence in the facility put her coworkers' lives at risk, therefore they decided to have her take another two-week leave of absence and continue to assess any developments as they occurred. Additionally, the company offered to transfer Diane to a facility around 100 miles away in a very large city where the company had many different campuses making it very difficult for Jim to find her. Diane turned down the transfer offer.

Week 9: During this two-week leave of absence, Jim got a message to Diane through a friend, telling her "he could not go through another divorce; one of them would have to die." The company decided to continue to have off-duty police officers in their facility and give Diane another two-week leave of absence.

Week 11: Diane reported that she had again been contacted by Jim through a friend who explained that Jim was now in psychological counseling and he was requesting that Diane join him in the sessions. Diane stated that she intended to go to the therapy sessions with him. The company advised her that she might want to contact the psychologist to verify that he was in counseling and ask the psychologist to reveal that he had come seeking therapy for his anger and violent tendencies rather than merely seeking marriage counseling. The company also continued her leave of absence.

Week 13: Diane revealed that she has been to two counseling sessions with Jim and felt safe to be around him. She also stated that Jim informed her that he would be retiring as he felt that his job added too much stress to his life and triggered some of his rage. Diane reported that her intention was to continue to go to counseling with Jim for another month, and if everything went well, she would move back into their home. The company advised her that she might want to check with the human resource department at Jim's employer to verify that he had notified them of his decision to retire. Diane's leave of absence was extended as the company continued to feel that her presence at the workplace endangered her coworkers.

Week 18: Diane reported that she had moved back in with Jim and would like to return to work. The company responded by offering her a cash severance package in exchange for her resignation.

This case study exemplifies several important points: The first is that these situations are sometimes with you for a long period of time. This case took four and a half months to work through. The second point is the concept of managing the fear of people within the organization. There was good reason for them to be afraid of Jim. He had many prior exhibitions of violence and rage; he had many encounters with the police to the point that the threat of notifying the authorities no longer had any effect on his actions; and he had made a direct threat to bring violence to their facility: "If I can't get to Diane then I will come down there and get Ray…" There was genuine fear of Jim and therefore, they did not want Diane back at the workplace.

One of the questions that will frequently arise during the discussion of this case regards the fairness of offering a severance package to Diane in order to get her to leave the company. Our response is that it was not fair to ask her to leave the company. But it was also not fair to continue her employment and possibly put her coworkers' lives at risk. It was not fair for her coworkers to suffer the continued anxiety of wondering when Jim's temper might flair up again. It was also not fair for the company to be put in the position of having to make this decision. But sometimes life is not fair, and in this situation, there were no good options to be found, so the company chose the option that benefited the majority of their employees. It was not a great option, but there were no great options available and the severance package was the best option available at the time.

OBSERVABLE SYMPTOMS OF RELATIONSHIP VIOLENCE

Because relationship violence is the most prevalent type of workplace violence that your organization may experience, it is important for you to know the observable symptoms that may be present in the victim's behavior. As a cautionary note, however, on any given day, anyone may exhibit these symptoms for a variety of reasons that have nothing to do with being the victim of relationship abuse. What you are looking for are negative, sustained changes in their behavior and not merely acute behavioral anomalies because of someone was having a bad day. Not surprisingly, many of these symptoms are also present as the symptoms of depression.

1. **Fatigue, tardiness, or unexplained absences.** The abuse, be it verbal or physical, frequently occurs at night and is often alcohol infused. It may begin at midnight or 1 a.m. and last for an hour or longer. When the abuser falls asleep, the victim is racked with fear and adrenaline and cannot easily fall asleep. Once the alarm clock goes off, the victim may have had less than two hours sleep and this will manifest itself in either being very groggy at work, being late, or being absent from work altogether.

2. **Withdrawing from interactions with other employees.** The victim of relationship abuse is frequently very near a breakdown and a

simple question from a coworker such as, "How are you doing?" can be all it takes for the victim to collapse in tears. To defend themselves from a breakdown, they erect emotional walls and create emotional and sometimes physical distance from their work associates.

3. **Exhibiting low self-esteem.** The abuser has inundated the victim with negative messages that the victim is worthless, stupid, unable to make decisions, unable to handle his or her own finances, and couldn't survive without the abuser. These messages, coupled with the victim's perceived inability to escape from the relationship, can be a severe detriment to the victim's self-esteem.

4. **Not taking a lunch break.** There can be several reasons for not taking a lunch break. The victim may lack an appetite caused by the abuse or fatigue. The victim may not take a lunch break because he or she doesn't want to be around other employees as noted in point 1. And the victim may not take a lunch break as the abuser is controlling the household finances and is not giving the victim the funds to buy a lunch or prepare a lunch at home.

5. **Receiving frequent cell phone calls that cause the employee to leave the work area.** There are usually two reasons for leaving the work area to take a call. Victims don't want coworkers to overhear the abuser yelling and/or the victim doesn't want coworkers to see him or her crying.

6. **Visible bruises or attempting to conceal bruises.** Concealment techniques may include the use of too much makeup over the affected areas, wearing jackets or other out-of-place garments to cover the bruises, or wearing sunglasses to conceal a black eye.

There are many reasons why someone might be skipping lunches or have a visible bruise that don't involve domestic abuse, so we would like to reiterate that you should be *observant of these symptoms as clusters of sustained changes to the person's normal behavior.*

DISCUSSING YOUR CONCERNS WITH THE ASSOCIATE

Once you have observed an employee or associate exhibiting sustained clusters of the aforementioned changes to his or her behavior, you will want to try assist. There are steps that you should consider as well as things to avoid. First, do not allude to the fact that you feel that your employee or associate is in an abusive relationship. They may be inclined to deny it, they may be embarrassed by it, and you may be completely wrong. Even if they are in an abusive relationship, they may go home and tell the abuser about your allegation, which may put you in a precarious position. Also, keep the discussion focused on helping them and do not imply that there are any disciplinary implications from this discussion unless the behaviors are violating your organization's policies or unless the behaviors have resulted in documented degradation of their work performance. Keep the discussion focused on the behaviors and do not mention any conclusions that you have drawn regarding the cause of those behaviors.

Work with other professionals in your organization, such as human resources or benefits, to draft a script and list the resources that are available through your employee assistance program (EAP) or other counseling services available through your organization or within your local community. Become familiar with your script but do not have the script in front of you when you meet with the person. You want your genuine concern to come through and that is somewhat difficult if you are frequently glancing down at a script or bullet points on a sheet of paper.

When you commence your meeting, a great way to start it off is by asking this question: "If I were to have a concern about you, you would want me to talk to you about it, wouldn't you?" The person will undoubtedly say "yes," and now you can list the behaviors that have caught your attention and explain why they have caused you to be concerned (e.g. "You've been coming in late quite a bit"; "You no longer come to our service anniversary luncheons"; and "You seem to be purposefully shying away from everyone else in the office."). Use positive statements to build the employee or associate up (e.g. "You're a valued member of our organization," etc.). Explain to the employee or associate that there are many reasons why someone may be exhibiting the behaviors you have noticed and your organization has options that have been successful in helping other people. List the benefits from your EAP or other counseling options, explain how to take advantage of the programs that are available, and even offer to call one of those options right then, giving the employee or associate time to talk one on one with an intake counselor. There are likely three outcomes to this conversation:

1. They may take you up on your offer and may or may not admit that they are involved in an abusive relationship.
2. They may tell you that their behavior is due to some other cause, such as the death of a close family member, and still take you up on your offer.
3. They many deny that they need any help whatsoever.

Even if option 3 is all you get, you should remind them that you were expressing your concern for them and that your "door is always open."

They may come back and take you up on your offer at a later point. Always remember that you should continually stress that the reason for this conversation is to help them.

ENDNOTES

[1] Robert Pearl, "Domestic Violence: The Secret Killer That Costs $8.3 Billion Annually," Forbes
http://www.forbes.com/sites/robertpearl/2013/12/05/domestic-violence-the-secret-killer-that-costs-8-3-billion-annually/

[2] S. Catalano, E. Smith, H. Snyder, and M. Rand, "Female Victims of Violence," modified Oct. 23, 2009, U.S. Department of Justice, Office of Justice Programs, Bureau of Justice Statistics: Selected Findings
http://bjs.ojp.usdoj.gov/content/pub/pdf/fvv.pdf

[3] "Adverse Health Conditions and Health Risk Behaviors Associated with Intimate Partner Violence – United States, 2005," *Morbidity and Mortality Weekly Report*, 57, no. 5 (Feb. 8, 2008): 113–117
http://www.cdc.gov/mmwr/preview/mmwrhtml/mm5705a1.htm

[4] S. Catalano, "Intimate Partner Violence in the United States," 2007, U.S. Department of Justice, Bureau of Justice Statistics
http://www.postandcourier.com/tilldeath/assets/d1-11.pdf

[5] National Center for Injury Prevention and Control, *Costs of Intimate Partner Violence Against Women in the United States* (Atlanta, GA: Centers for Disease Control and Prevention, 2003)
http://www.cdc.gov/violenceprevention/pdf/IPVBook-a.pdf

CHAPTER 6

Associate Violence

"A 'snapshot' feature in USA Today *listed the five greatest concerns parents and teachers had about children in the '50s: talking out of turn, chewing gum in class, doing homework, stepping out of line, cleaning their rooms. Then it listed the five top concerns of parents today: drug addiction, teenage pregnancy, suicide and homicide, gang violence, anorexia and bulimia. ... Between my own childhood and the advent of my motherhood—one short generation—the culture had gone completely mad."*

—Mary Kay Blakely, author and Associate Professor Emerita,
University of Missouri School of Journalism

Contents

Abstract

All organizations have a risk of violence in the workplace and all have the ability to see the various warning signal behaviors that occur prior to that violence, provided the perpetrators are known to the organization. When an organization builds a program designed to prevent violence, it must ensure that the goal is to detect these behaviors early enough to allow for proper management of the situation. The vast majority of the cases of violence or threats of violence in the workplace are not the highly publicized mass shooting cases, which are few, but rather they are the more common stalking, harassing, and intimidating behaviors that can lead to violence. These actions must be treated as precursors to violence and not allowed to persist. Far too often organizations tolerate or overlook disturbing behavior only to have it erupt in actual violence. Becoming well versed in the warning behaviors of those moving toward violence is a significant step toward preventing that violence.

Keywords: addiction; behavioral warning signs; disturbing behavior; emotionally attached employee; mass shootings; multiple homicide; outbursts of rage; red flag behaviors; revenge; snapped; suicide; threatening behavior; troubled associate; violence, workplace shootings; written manifesto

"He just snapped; there was nothing we could have done." Frequently this has been the sound bite that that survivors of workplace shootings and the coworkers, friends, and family of the shooter offer to the news media after a multiple workplace homicide occurs. This rationalization may make them feel better, but there were undoubtedly noticeable and escalating changes in the shooter's behavior indicating trouble was on the way. Either no one paid attention or they didn't know who to talk to about their observations. One of the benefits of the constant media coverage of these multiple homicides is that the news media continues to cover the investigation and trial of the shooter and people see that there were red flag behaviors that were missed and the shooter did not just snap—there was a lot of planning put into the tragic actions of the shooter.

As an example, let's review one of the worst shooting rampages in U.S. history, which is the shooting at the Virginia Polytechnic Institute and State

University (Virginia Tech) campus. On April 16, 2007, 23-year-old Seung-Hui Cho killed 32 people before taking his own life.

The seeds of this tragic event, however, had been growing for several years. Sixteen months prior to the shooting, on December 13, 2005, Cho was ordered into outpatient treatment by a judge after it was reported that he had been making suicidal statements to his roommates. Cho's angry and often violent writing for class assignments worried both professors and students alike. He was released after a mental health facility's evaluation cleared him of being a risk to himself or anyone else.

On February 9, 2007, Cho purchased a 0.22 caliber pistol at a local gun shop. One month later Cho purchased a 9 mm pistol and ammunition at a different gun shop.

On April 16, 2007, Cho entered a campus dormitory and shot one female and one male student. He then proceeded to the post office where he mailed a package to NBC News in New York that contained a video, photographs, and his written manifesto. He then proceeded to a classroom building, chained the doors shut, and began his shooting rampage, killing 32 students and professors and wounding 20 more prior to turning the gun on himself and taking his own life. Cho's video and manifesto showed that he harbored a grievance toward "wealthy brats." The subsequent investigation did not show any evidence that Cho knew any of his victims. [1], [2], [3]

Although this is a very high-level view of the events preceding and occurring during the rampage shooting, it does demonstrate that Cho had mental health problems for at least two years prior to the shooting that had not been completely addressed. He had issues with anger and violent ideology that students and professors knew about, but that knowledge never made its way to anyone who would be in a position to help. Cho meticulously planned out his day of rage, making videos, taking photographs, and writing his manifesto. He researched and made choices about which firearms to purchase, and he learned that he could increase his body count by chaining the doors closed and keeping law enforcement's first responders at bay.

Before we proceed, we wish to state that the goal of any organization's violence prevention program should not be to terminate associates for "crossing the line" or to prosecute them later if they act out in an unlawful manner. *The goal of your program is the early identification of the troubled associate and getting that associate the help he or she needs or removing that associate from the organization before he or she becomes emotionally attached to the job.* Early identification and intervention is a key component of your program as shown in our next case study.

Robert was the regional director for his company and the top executive working out of the company's regional office. Robert was an experienced executive having worked his way up in the company over the past 16 years. Robert's experience gave him confidence that he could handle pretty much anything that came up. That feeling of confidence was about to be shattered.

As usual Robert arrived before most of the other people. He came into his office with a cup of hot coffee, settled into his desk, checked his appointments for the day, and logged into his email to clear up some overnight correspondence. One of the emails came from outside the company, having later been determined as being sent from an Internet café. This anonymous email stated that Janice, an employee in the accounts receivable department, went into an angry rage yesterday afternoon and stabbed two holes in the department manager's door. Robert thought this to be absurd and determined that someone must be trying to get Janice in trouble. Janice had worked there for more than seven years with acceptable performance reviews and Robert had never heard of any complaints being lodged against her. Nonetheless Robert got on the elevator and headed down four levels to the department where Janice worked because his company had a policy that all complaints had to be investigated, even the anonymous ones that are thought to be unfounded.

When Robert walked into the accounts receivable department, he saw that Janice was one of the few employees to have arrived. Jeff, the department manager, had not come in yet and his door was still closed. Robert went over to Jeff's office and became a little unsettled when he saw that there were two deep puncture holes in the door.

Robert then went to Janice's cubicle and asked her if she knew what made the two holes. Janice replied that she did know and stated that she was so mad at Jeff yesterday afternoon that she grabbed a screwdriver with the intent of stabbing him in the neck. Upon seeing that Jeff had left for the day Janice decided to "take it out on his door." It was at that point that Robert's confidence abandoned him. Nothing in his 16 years on the job had prepared him to handle this type of an incident. Robert did know enough to immediately go to the human resource department who initiated a full investigation.

The investigators began interviewing other employees and reviewing Janice's personnel records. They found that statements given by witnesses of Janice's behavior were in stark contrast to the documents in her personnel file. The investigators found that while Janice had worked there for seven years, her coworkers had been deathly afraid of her for the past five. A year or so after she came on board, Janice began to become irritable. She balked at some of the assignments she was given and openly spoke about her disapproval of her managers. Her verbal behavior began to escalate and people shied away from her as she frequently unleashed a torrid wave of obscenities at the slightest provocation. She began to accuse others, usually the managers, for sabotaging her work. She became enraged if office supplies were out of place when she went looking for them or if someone inadvertently removed one of her documents from the printer. Her behavior then escalated from being verbally abusive to physically threatening. Janice would frequently throw things like staplers or tape dispensers when she was angry. The investigators were shown several file cabinet drawers that would not close properly because Janice had slammed them so hard, so many times. The employees interviewed also identified at least eight coworkers who allegedly left because of Janice's behavior.

Her personnel files, conversely, were devoid of any mention of any such conduct. There were no disciplinary warnings and her annual performance reviews were all satisfactory in nature with no noted behavioral problems. It was also noted that Janice seemed to have been frequently transferred from department to department. On interview, her present and past department managers stated that they all knew of Janice's temper and behavior, but they were too afraid to discipline her for them. Whenever things began to boil over, rather than address the issues, she was transferred to another department. In fact, the investigation uncovered that occasionally the job she was transferred into was at a higher pay grade than the job she came from so, in effect, Janice was being financially rewarded for terrorizing the workplace.

Even though there were no prior disciplinary actions taken with Janice, the company was adamant that she had "crossed the line" and had to go. Terminating her, however, was not without risk. During her discussion with the investigators, she told them that she frequently blacked out during her outbursts of rage and had no idea what she had just done. She also related that she occasionally had thoughts of suicide and that her job was the only stable influence in her life.

So Janice needed to go, but how best to do it? How do you soften the blow in such a sensitive case? Here's what the company did: Janice was put on a medical leave and voluntarily entered counseling under the company's Employee Assistance Program. After six weeks of counseling, the psychologist felt that Janice was stable enough to face her separation from the company. The company met Janice in the conference room of a hotel near her home. They explained that she was being terminated and was given a modest severance check with a guarantee that the company would pay for her next six months of counseling sessions. This was certainly a generous plan, but Janice was extremely upset. Her complaint, and rightfully so, was that she had been with the company for more than seven years and during that time, no one had ever told her that her behavior was inappropriate and might cause her to lose her job. Her department manager's tacit response to her behavior was tantamount to acceptance. Her displeasure with the termination did not result in an outburst of rage but she was extremely and visibly upset—so much so that for the next three months, the company paid for off-duty police officers to sit in a conference room just off the main lobby in case Janice returned.

The preceding case is perhaps the best example of how *not* to handle a disruptive associate. So many issues were mishandled that they compounded the problems and exemplified the adage that "ignoring problems does not make them go away, it only makes them bigger," or as we like to say, "Negligence is the fertilizer that grows big problems out of small ones." This case also exemplifies the reason for identifying problems early: They are easier to handle when they are small problems. Had a department manager addressed Janice's behavior when she first verbally lashed out, she would have at least been on notice that her behavior was inappropriate, she would have had the opportunity to identify the actions that were inappropriate, and she could have striven to improve her demeanor. If she could not reign in her temper, then perhaps she could have been encouraged to enter anger management counseling through the company's Employee Assistance Program. If she did not take advantage of the counseling program, then at lease the diligent ongoing disciplinary action from her manager could have brought the matter to a conclusion before five more years passed—and before Janice attained a strong emotional attachment to the job, before her actions became physically threatening, and before eight or so coworkers left the business because they could not stand the stress of one more day in the office with her.

With Janice's case in mind, as well as the Virginia Tech shooting and the other case studies from the previous chapters, let's take a closer look at the behaviors and motives that you should be cognizant of in the attitudes and actions of those within your organization.

One of the first things to mention is that you are looking for changes, usually negative, in a person's behavior. No one commits a mass murder on his or her first day of work, so similarly, no one exhibits disruptive, threatening behavior on his or her first day of work either. Cho was at Virginia Tech for well over a year before his behavior escalated into a shooting rampage and Janice was working at her place of employment for about two years when people first noticed a negative change in her behavior. The changes in behavior will be noticeable to anyone who is paying attention.

Another important note is that many of these motives and behaviors can be intertwined. For example, the motive may be revenge, but it can be expressed by outbursts of rage or even in subtler behaviors, such as absenteeism and/or poor work performance. Finally, the behaviors and motives described in the following section are also present in the perpetrators who we classify as external threats, so keep these in mind as you read the next chapter.

MOTIVE AND BEHAVIORAL WARNING SIGNS

Revenge. One of the most common motives is revenge. [4] Perhaps the person has experienced the end of a relationship, abandonment by friends, and disciplinary action at work or the loss of a job. Whatever the real or perceived snub, the perpetrator's notion of a grievance with someone, some people, or at the organization as a whole can give him or her cause to plot revenge. In some situations the grievance is minor and blown out of proportion by the perpetrator. However, grievances dealing with the workplace—real or otherwise—should never be ignored. Feeling that no one will listen or that no one cares can often escalate the perpetrator's mood and actions. By giving the grievance a proper and serious airing, they may feel that at least the organization gave them their "day in court" even if the determination did not go in their favor. Occasionally we will have an organization relate that they do not like to hear petty grievances or grievances that they know are either false or blown out of proportion because it only encourages the person or others within the organization to file frivolous claims. First, these organizations are making the determination that the claim is frivolous without due diligence, which, at best, may be a violation of collective bargaining agreements as well as state and federal regulations regarding employee grievances, whistleblowing, and ethics. Second, we would much prefer to have someone filing claims than shooting up our facility. As long as they are filing claims, they at least still have faith in the grievance process. The lesson to learn here is that your organization should have a well-publicized grievance program.

Attendance problems. The first place that potential trouble can be spotted is in someone who suddenly develops attendance problems. If workers are being bullied at work, they may not show up the next day. If workers are upset with a coworker, they may not show up the next day. If workers are upset with a supervisor or with the company in general, they may not show up the next day. In short, if someone has any anxiety about being there, he or she may not show up to work. Additionally, failure to come to work can also be the first sign of someone taking revenge on the organization. If workers don't come to work, then their assignments have to be shifted to other coworkers. Everyone in the department will suffer and the productivity of the work group is diminished.

Sometimes attendance problems are indicative of abuse at home as discussed in Chapter 5. Sometimes attendance problems are the result of substance abuse. Last, attendance problems can also occur if the person has developed a chronic illness. All of this means that if someone's attendance has become problematic then find out why and see what can be done to help.

Negative changes in work performance. Over time there can become a marked change from acceptable or even good work performance to unacceptable or poor performance. This can also go hand in hand with attendance problems. If someone is frequently absent, then his or her workload is backing up.

Revenge can also be a factor in poor work performance. The worker might be slowing down because he or she wants to make the supervisor or even the entire work group look bad to company executives.

Poor work performance can also be a result of someone who feels overcome by the job or overwhelmed with life, and is questioning why he or she should continue with either. These are all indications that the person may be in crisis. Poor work performance should be addressed to find out and resolve the reasons for the negative change in work performance.

Withdrawal from others in the organization. When workers who had normal, healthy social relationships with their coworkers and supervisors suddenly withdraw from them, there is a problem. It may be that there is a problem at home or it may be that there is a problem at work, but there is a problem, and as we learned in the case with Janice, it is much harder to resolve problems when you ignore them and give them time to grow; they are much easier to address when they are in their earlier stages.

Negative changes in appearance and hygiene. If someone used to be attired in clothing appropriate for your business but begins to dress down, perhaps wearing the same clothing several days in a row, perhaps wearing t-shirts with graphics and verbiage that are inappropriate for your organization and are insensitive to coworkers, then something has changed in this person's emotions. A further symptom is negative changes in the worker's hygiene: Perhaps the worker let his or her hair grow out and did not bother to comb or style it before coming to work. Another frequent symptom is failure to bathe at appropriate intervals or failure to bathe at all. This is all indicative of something changing for the worse in the life of the worker, and needless to say, this is behavior that needs to be looked into and not ignored.

Feeling that someone or everyone in the organization is out to get him or her. Feelings of persecution are warning signs that need to be heeded. This is an indication that the person's reality has changed and he or she might become chronically irrational. This is also a time to make sure that the worker is not harboring an unheard grievance. If the worker has a grievance that the supervisor ignored, this can fuel the notion that the supervisor is out to get the worker and eventually lead the worker to believe that the organization, as a whole, is out to somehow hurt him or her or sabotage his or her career. These unresolved feelings could escalate into outbursts of rage and escalate even further to the person causing damage to the organization's property during the rage. This is a particularly dangerous situation as the next escalation of the behavior usually involves someone being harmed. It might be an intentional assault or collateral damage that occurred during the rage, but the result is the same: someone got hurt on your premises because of someone's actions that were not appropriately addressed and you failed to protect the injured party.

Addiction. Whether it is abuse of alcohol or drugs, we have frequently seen addiction in the background of those who have perpetrated threats or violence. Addiction can also be a reason for attendance problems, work performance issues, and negative changes in appearance and hygiene. Further, the abuse of drugs and alcohol can also repress a person's inhibitions and prompt the worker to say and do things that he or she would not do when in a sober state. Substance abuse can also disrupt the brain's chemistry and escalate behavior toward rage and violence. Regardless, time and time again, we have seen enough problems with addiction to know that alcohol and drug abuse is a trap that from which the addicts cannot free themselves from without help. They may not accept your help, but you owe it to the addict, your coworkers, and your organization to try.

Easily angered escalating to outbursts of rage. We have already discussed anger and rage as a part of other behaviors, but we note it here as its own symptom because it may be the first action of which people take serious notice.

Violent and/or suicidal ideation. This ideation can be expressed verbally, in writing, or in social media posts and contains expressions of the satisfaction the worker will feel when he or she takes their violent revenge, or the regret, sorrow, and guilt that the worker will feel when he or she takes his or her own life. In many instances the individual wants others to see and understand these feelings so this information may be easily discoverable.

Contextually inappropriate interest in firearms and/or explosives and recent acquisition of multiple weapons. [5] There are those who view anyone who owns a firearm with suspicion. We don't want to enter into a political debate, but we do want to make a point. There are approximately 90 million adult gun owners in the United States versus approximately 113,000 acts of gun violence annually. [6], [7], [8] Please do not misunderstand us, we are not inferring that 113,000 acts of gun violence is an acceptable level; it is not. The point we are trying to make is if you paint every gun owner with the same broad brush of suspicion, you will not be able to hone in on identifying those who present a real risk. The difference is the context in which their interest in firearms is presented. If they talk about firearms in the context of hunting; trap and skeet shooting, or other competitions; recreational target shooting; or even self-defense, they are not showing any indications of violence toward another person regardless of whether you personally find those activities to your liking. There are even organized groups who obtain period firearms and uniforms and reenact every U.S. military campaign from the Revolutionary War to World War II. Conversely, if the associate's conversations about firearms dwell on death with violent verbal imagery about the potential injuries the firearms can cause, then there is reason for concern. Simply stated in another fashion, if their conversation about firearms would cause a reasonable person to feel intimidated, then this requires your follow-up. .

Contextually inappropriate and intense interest or fascination with previous active shootings or mass attacks. [5] It is commonly known that many shooters in the planning stages of their own shooting rampages have studied other mass murderers. One recent example is Adam Lanza, who killed 27 people and injured 2 more in the 2012 shooting at the Sandy Hook Elementary School. He was found to have been obsessed with many of the prior mass murders that took place in recent history, such as:

- The 1999 Columbine High School shooting, which left 15 dead and 24 injured
- The 2006 Amish school shooting in Nickel Mines, Pennsylvania, where 6 died and 5 were wounded
- The 2008 Northern Illinois University murders, which took the lives of 6 people and injured 21 more
- The 2011 mass murders in Norway, which killed 71 people and injured 241 [9]

Troubled individuals who harbor such obsessions do not publicize them widely, however, they are not kept top secret either. Evidence of these obsessions are observable should anyone take notice. We will discuss this further in Chapter 7.

Extreme recklessness with finances or in sexual encounters with a complete disregard of future consequences. [5] This explanation is fairly obvious and it is also means that the person has reached a dangerous point in his or her behavior escalation. These people have given up on any resolution for their real or perceived problems, and they have resolved themselves to the notion that violence, either to themselves or others, is how their troubles will end. As such, they may irrationally spend or give away money or other assets and engage in promiscuous and unprotected sexual encounters.

Documenting their rationale in a written manifesto. In the post-incident investigation of mass murders, it is sometimes unclear what prompted the perpetrators to commit their heinous crimes. Others, however, want the world to know why and sometimes they are hoping to spark some type of movement to effect social change. Virginia Tech's Cho documented his manifesto in writing, video, and photographs and sent it off to NBC News. Anders Breivik, who perpetrated the tragic killings in Norway, left a 1500-page manifesto. Dylann Roof who killed nine parishioners at the Mother Emanuel A.M.E. Church in 2015 left his manifesto in the form of a website. And the worst mass murderer in history got his manifesto published as a book—Adolf Hitler's *Mein Kampf*, which is still available at bookstores today.

As we end this chapter, it is important to make two important notes:

1. When we discuss behaviors that may be indications of future troubled behavior and possible violence, we should be looking for clusters of negative and sustained changes in the individual's normative behavior. On any given day, anyone of us might temporarily exhibit one or more of the aforementioned behaviors because of some stress factor that we are experiencing and from which we will recover fairly quickly.

2. Although these aforementioned behaviors are a good guideline of warning signs, the list should not be considered to be complete. If we were to declare this list to be the final word on disturbing behavior, there would be an event in the near future that would uncover additional symptoms not recognized in any prior workplace violence event. Assessing threatening behavior cannot be done via a checklist, as every case will have differences. The best advice to give is to note any behavior that seems troublesome, whether it is on this list or not, and then investigate the reasons for and the implications of the behavior.

ENDNOTES

[1] "Massacre at Virginia Tech Leaves 32 Dead," This Day In History
    http://www.history.com/this-day-in-history/massacre-at-virginia-tech-leaves-32-dead
[2] "Virginia Tech Shooting Fast Facts," CNN Library
    http://www.cnn.com/2013/10/31/us/virginia-tech-shootings-fast-facts/

[3] Julia Glum, "Virginia Tech Shooting Anniversary: How the 2007 Massacre Changed the Safety on College Campuses," *International Business Times,* April 15, 2015, http://www.ibtimes.com/virginia-tech-shooting-anniversary-how-2007-massacre-changed-safety-college-campuses-1883642

[4] A. Hempel, J. Meloy, and T. Richards, *Offender and Offense Characteristics of a Nonrandom Sample of Mass Murders, American Academy of Psychiatry and the Law,* 27, no. 2, 1999.

[5] *Active Shooter Planning and Response in a Healthcare Setting,* Healthcare and Public Sector Coordinating Council, April 2015 https://www.fbi.gov/about-us/cirg/active-shooter-and-mass-casualty-incidents/active-shooter-planning-and-response-in-a-healthcare-setting

[6] "A Profile of Gun Owners," PEW Research Center, March 12, 2013 http://www.people-press.org/2013/03/12/section-3-gun-ownership-trends-and-demographics/#profile-guns

[7] People QuickFacts, United States Census Bureau, http://quickfacts.census.gov/qfd/states/00000.html

[8] Dewey G. Cornell, "Gun Violence and Mass Shootings: Myths, Facts and Solutions," *Washington Post,* June 11, 2014 http://www.washingtonpost.com/news/the-watch/wp/2014/06/11/gun-violence-and-mass-shootings-myths-facts-and-solutions/

[9] Tom Winter, Hannah Rappleye, Monica Alba, and Kristen Dhalgren, "Police Release Full Newtown Massacre Report, with Photos and Video," NBC News, December 27, 2013 http://investigations.nbcnews.com/_news/2013/12/27/21736461-police-release-full-newtown-massacre-report-with-photos-and-video?lite

CHAPTER 7

External Violence

"Never trust to general impressions, my boy, but concentrate yourself upon details."
—*Arthur Conan Doyle,* The Adventures of Sherlock Holmes

Contents

Abstract

External threats to any organization generally fall into two categories: (1) those who have made their threat known, and (2) those who have not. In both cases these people will give off warning signals prior to acts of violence. If an organization recognizes what risk they have by the virtue of the nature of their business or significance to certain groups, they can take steps to mitigate the risks from all external sources. Many organizations see this and take proper security measures anticipating such a threat. Additionally they should develop threat assessment and management programs to help determine if external threats are moving toward violence. Several recent cases of such external threat violence have highlighted the need for a combination of sound security practices and assessment skills.

Keywords: escalated behavior; external threat; grievance; Holocaust Museum; manifesto; mass violence; rampage shooters; revenge; social withdrawal; suicidal ideation; targeted organization; violence; warning flag

In the realm of violence from external sources we generally see two types of threats. Those coming from individuals who have made their grievance and/or their threats of revenge known to their targeted organization and those who seemingly fly under the radar. Both types certainly do exhibit warning signs but, in the latter type, those signs will usually not be exhibited to their target(s). Let's start with those who make their grievance and threats know to the organization.

The warning behaviors for individuals making external threats are similar to those listed in Chapter 6, "Associate Violence." Although the behaviors are listed here, please refer to Chapter 6 for a fuller discussion of their descriptions:

- Revenge
- Withdrawal from social connections
- Negative changes in appearance and hygiene
- Belief that the targeted organization is responsible for all of his or her problems
- Addiction
- Easily angered
- Violent and/or suicidal ideation
- Contextually inappropriate interest in firearms and/or explosives and recent acquisition of multiple weapons
- Contextually inappropriate fascination of prior acts of mass violence
- Extreme recklessness with own personal life with no regard to the potential consequences
- Preparation of a manifesto

Let's now review an example of how these warning signs can manifest themselves.

The concerning behaviors will be printed in **bold** as they occur in the following case study.

James J. Lee was a man with a cause. Lee had long been an environmentalist, but after watching Al Gore's documentary, *An Inconvenient Truth*, he felt that the world as he knew it was teetering on the brink of extinction. So Lee contacted the corporate headquarters of the Discovery Channel located in a suburb near Washington, D.C. Lee tried to convince the broadcaster to produce more programming dedicated to showing how humans were destroying the planet and the necessity of strict environmental and population controls. He even pitched them a *Save the Planet* reality game show. His pitches fell on deaf ears. This was his **grievance.**

Lee continued to send the Discovery Channel letters, wrote emails, and even put up a website dedicated to his cause where he stated: "If their 'environmental' shows are actually working, then why is the news about the environment getting worse? It should be getting better if they were doing their job and we should be seeing that reflected on the nightly news. But NO! The Discovery Channel is actually not about saving the planet; they are just another 'green' corporation whose real interests lie in MONEY! Products! Junk! Trash!" Thus, his **manifesto** became public.

When these pursuits failed, Lee **escalated his behavior** by traveling to the Discovery Channel headquarters, where he began daily protest outside of their offices. Many people at the Discovery Channel failed to see any potential danger in Lee's escalated actions. Nathaniel Harrington, a former Discovery employee, told MSNBC's Peter Alexander, "He was seen as something of a joke." Harrington went on, "I hate to say it, but at the time we kind of half-joked about it because he could come back shooting. Nobody took it very seriously."[1] Even though the organization saw no danger in Lee, he was eventually arrested as his behavior escalated and turned **reckless, showing no regard for the potential consequences,** when he began throwing thousands of dollars in the air, which attracted a crowd that quickly became unruly as they scrambled for the cash. He was sentenced to six months of supervised probation for this disturbance and ordered to stay away from the Discovery Channel's offices.

All of this culminated in Lee's final act of **revenge** on September 1, 2010, when he entered the building with what turned out to be starter pistols and several explosive devices. When Lee entered the building, he fired one of the starter pistols into the air. As would be expected, confusion reigned because the company was not prepared for an act of violence on their premises. "Someone over the P.A. said there's a situation in the lobby, go back to your desks," Melissa Shepard, a Discovery employee, told MSNBC TV. "So we all went to offices and crammed into offices and shut the lights off and listened to the news. Then someone knocked on the door and said we need to evacuate." Shepard described initial confusion over the evacuation plan. "The scariest was when they were telling us to go upstairs, then downstairs, then upstairs. I don't know if it was safe," she said. "The thing is we were hearing there were two people, then explosives, then hostages, then that people were shot. We kept hearing different stories. It was one thing after another."[1]

Several hours into the standoff Lee was shot and killed by the police.

The Discovery Channel was lucky that no employees were physically injured. Undoubtedly there were psychological injuries, some of which are probably still being treated.

We are sure that the Discovery Channel, like most broadcasters, receives a multitude of letters amounting to unsolicited pitches for programming. It is probably not feasible to respond to them. However, Lee's appearance at the company's headquarters and daily picketing should have been a huge red warning flag. An appropriate course of action would have been to increase security while bringing in threat assessment and management professionals to begin an investigation into Lee's background (which would have discovered his online manifesto), gather his prior correspondence for analysis, note his continued and escalating behaviors, develop an intervention plan, and make sure Discovery had taken all possible precautions to include the training of their employees on what to do if an act of violence occurred in the building or on the premises.

The Discovery Channel incident is an example of a situation where warning signs were present but ignored, allowing the disturbing behaviors of one individual to escalate into physical violence putting the lives of people within the organization at risk. There are also times when warning signs are there, but not visible to people within the organization. Let's look at one such example and see how the events unfolded.

Paul Ciancia was raised in New Jersey. He was considered a loner, and there are some who report that he was bullied while in school. Ciancia trained to be a motorcycle mechanic and was being groomed by his father to one-day take over the family body shop. However, Ciancia decided to move to Los Angeles. At some time during his tenure in Los Angeles, he became dissatisfied with the federal government as he felt the government was becoming too complicit to the "New World Order," a notion held by some conspiracy theorists that a one-world government is emerging.

In late October 2013, he began telling his roommates that he might need a ride to the airport as his father was ailing. On November 1, he sent a text message to his brother and sister stating that he intended to harm himself. They contacted their local police department who, in turn, notified the Los Angeles Police Department (LAPD). The LAPD dispatched officers to conduct a wellness check only to find that one of Ciancia's roommates had just taken him to the airport, as Ciancia had stated that he wanted to fly back to New Jersey to visit his father.

At 9:30 a.m., Ciancia entered terminal 3 at Los Angeles International Airport with a bag containing a rifle and several hundred rounds of ammunition. He approached the first Transportation Security Administration (TSA) passenger identification post at the bottom of an escalator whereupon he took the rifle out of the bag and shot TSA Officer Gerardo Hernandez in the chest. Hernandez later succumbed to his wounds before he could be taken to the hospital. Ciancia then proceeded up the escalator, where passengers and airport personnel were fleeing and finding places to hide. He casually walked down the unsecured concourse, occasionally stopping to ask people if they were with the TSA. During this time, Ciancia shot and wounded two more TSA officers and one other person before airport police officers shot him four times.[2],[3]

These murders were almost prevented. If only a few minutes could have been shaved off of the time it took to communicate his suicidal text messages to law enforcement and if a few more minutes could have been shaved off the police response time, they might have been able to stop him before he left for the airport; they might have had time to look in his bag and taken him in for mental counseling. One of the denials we sometimes face in an organization is the mistaken notion that these events cannot be prevented. Nothing could be further from the truth. Part of this thinking is because violence that is prevented usually does not make the news media. In the rare instance when it is reported, it is given one mention, then disappears, as violence that did not occur is just not as newsworthy as a mass homicide. Violence, however, is prevented all the time as depicted in the following scenarios:

- Sisters and brother notice that a sibling has become withdrawn and depressed while also abusing drugs and alcohol. They intervene, thus saving the life of someone spiraling toward suicide.
- A partner or spouse sees that her significant other's anger is boiling over and erupting in outbursts of rage. She seeks refuge in a women's shelter, and the potential violence and possible death to her and/or her children is averted.
- Employees report escalating disruptive behavior of a coworker to an employer who intervenes and gets the disruptive employee into counseling, thereby preventing possible workplace violence.
- Neighbors report suspicious behavior on the part of some men in the neighborhood. A police investigation is conducted, and a cell of terrorists preparing for a mass murder is thwarted.

HOW MUCH SECURITY IS APPROPRIATE?

One of the reasons that the body count attained by Paul Ciancia was mitigated is because of the Los Angeles Airport has its own on-site police force that is trained for these kinds of situations. For more than five decades, airports have known that they are targets for hijackers, terrorists, and others with criminal intent. Most large airports all over the world are protected by highly trained and armed police officers or military detachments. This protection is expensive and out of the reach of many businesses. Fortunately, this level of security is not needed at most places.

Most organizations will only experience a short-term security threat, such as occurred at the Discovery Channel headquarters. If the warning signs are recognized, then intervention plans can be built to prevent violence, and security can be enhanced to mitigate the violence or thwart it from occurring. To do this effectively, there are four steps that must be executed:

1. The associates must be trained in what behaviors should be reported.
2. They must be provided and trained to use the organization's reporting process.
3. The organization must be trained to assess threating behavior and build intervention and security plans.
4. The organization must have prearranged security options that can be put in place within an hour or two of notice. Waiting until someone has threatened to come shoot a company executive is the wrong time to begin negotiating with a security company.

Early recognition and intervention are your best friends. Denial, rationalization, and apathy are your enemies. An expanded view of a comprehensive workplace violence program begins in the next chapter.

Conversely, there are organizations that are frequently targeted by the lone, mass murderer, such as Paul Ciancia, or by organized cells of terrorists. The goal of the domestic rampage shooter or a foreign terrorist organization is to produce a large body count and strike fear into the population. Frequently, the rampage shootings and terrorist attacks are conducted in the hope of sparking social or political change.

The Japanese sneak attack on Pearl Harbor was designed to knock out our ability to be a military power in the Pacific and therein cause us to end economic sanctions against Japan. From that standpoint, it failed.

Revolution was the desired result of the assassination of two Las Vegas police officers in June 2014. Jerad Miller and his wife Amanda shot and killed the two police officers who were having lunch at a pizza parlor, placing a note on one of them that stated, "The revolution has begun." The revolution ended a short while later when they exchanged gunfire with police inside the rear of Walmart. Amanda, apparently realizing that they were cornered, shot her husband twice before taking her own life.

Charles Manson directed the heinous Tate-LaBianca murders in 1969, believing it would spark a race war. This was also the intention of Dylann Roof when he went on his murder rampage at the church in Charleston, South Carolina, in June 2015. Neither Manson nor Roof's murders initiated a race war.

One of the intentions of the September 11, 2001 attacks was to convince the U.S. population and leaders to stay out of the Middle East. Obviously that goal was not achieved. It is a shame that these perpetrators do not pay attention to past history, because history tells us that whenever the country or segments of the population are attacked, it does not cause division or withdrawal, but brings unity and strengthens resolve.

Following is a list of some of the targets terrorists choose along with the goals they expect to achieve. In most instances the perpetrator(s) select targets that will help them attain several of their goals. Organizations falling into these categories require a heightened awareness and enhanced security measures.

- *Symbolic targets.* It was no coincidence that the September 11 attackers chose to hijack American and United Airlines planes, crashing them into the World Trade Center and the Pentagon. They wanted the people of the United States to know that this was an attack on us, our government, and military, and the center of our capitalist society.
- *Body count.* Body count is important beyond the perpetrator's lust for murder. Perpetrators also lust for infamy and the higher the body count, the more media attention will be garnered on them, and their place in history will be secure. This is why Eric Harris and Dylan Klebold chose Columbine High School, where they killed 15 and injured 24 people on April 20, 1999. This is one of the reasons why the September 11 attackers chose the World Trade Center, where they killed 2,996 people and injured another 6,000 on September 11, 2001. This one of the reasons Seung-Hui Cho chose Virginia Polytechnic Institute and State University (Virginia Tech), where he killed 33 people and injured 28 on April 16, 2007. This is why James Holmes chose the packed midnight preview showing of the latest *Batman* movie, when he killed 12 and injured 70 moviegoers at the Aurora, Colorado, Century movie theatre on July 20, 2012. This is the reason that Adam Lanza chose the Sandy Hook

Elementary School, where he killed 28 students and teachers and injured 2 more on December 14, 2012. It is also the reason that Dylann Roof selected the Emmanuel Methodist Episcopal in Charleston, South Carolina, on June 17, 2015 where he killed nine church members and injured one.

- *Children.* Nothing strikes fear deep in the collective hearts of a nation faster than the slaughter of the nation's youth. Currently, we have only endured attacks on children by the singular shooter or two shooters, as was the case at Columbine High School. However, school and school bus attacks by terrorist groups occur all too frequently in the Middle East and Africa. One of the most horrific cases ever occurred in Beslan, Russia, on September 1, 2004. Chechen separatist militants selected the first day of school to storm the Beslan School, taking 1,100 hostages of which 777 were children. They held the hostages for three days, perpetrating unspeakable horrors on their captives. On the third day of the standoff, Russian forces stormed the building with the eventual death toll standing at 385 lives. For an in-depth understanding of what happened in Beslan, we recommend interested readers obtain a copy of John Giduck's *Terror at Beslan: A Russian Tragedy with Lessons for American Schools.* If terrorists were able to coordinate mass murders at several schools across the country on the same day, think of the effect it would have. Schools would be closed indefinitely. Children across the nation would be traumatized. Parents would stay home from work to be with their children, causing an immediate effect on the American economy. This is why schools make tempting targets for terrorists.
- *Centers of government and military installations.* The September 11 attackers crashed American Airlines flight 77 into the Pentagon and United flight 93, which was downed by the hijackers after the passengers tried to take the plane back, was probably headed for a government building. Other examples would include the bombing of the Alfred P. Murrah Federal Building in Oklahoma City by Timothy McVeigh on April 19, 1995, which killed 168 and injured 600, and the shooting at Fort Hood Army Base in Texas on November 11, 2009, by Army Major Nidal Hasan, which killed 13 and injured 33 people.
- *Centers of business and finance.* The obvious example is the World Trade Center attack on September 11, 2001. However, there was also the 2013 Westgate Mall attack in Nairobi, Kenya, that left 60 people dead, and

in February 2015, extremist group Al Shabaab called for attacks on Minnesota's Mall of America as well as West Edmonton Mall in Canada and the Oxford Street Shopping Area in London.[4] If terrorists attacked the Mall of America, causing a mass murder of shoppers and storekeepers, it would fulfill several of their goals:

- With the name "Mall of America," it is certainly a symbolic target.
- With the size of the Mall of America, it is also a tourist destination and would provide the opportunity for a large body count, especially if attacked on a weekend or at a time near a holiday.
- Because of the amusement park in the center of the mall, there are frequently children on site and in numbers, meaning an attack there would strike fear in the hearts of parents across the country.
- Finally, malls across the country would close until additional security precautions could be taken. The temporary closure of the malls and the large number of employees left without an income would strike a blow to the economy. Once the malls reopened, it would take an indefinite period of time before customers would return to pre-attack levels, and parents would reevaluate their decisions to allow the mall to be their children's social destination.
- *Locations of religious or ideological significance.* This was the case on June 6, 2009, when James Wenneker von Brunn went to the United States Holocaust Museum in Washington, D.C. Von Brunn had a troubled past. In 1981, he was arrested at the Federal Reserve Building when he entered with several weapons intent on executing a citizen's arrest of the Reserve's board of governors.[5] Von Brunn was known to be a white supremacist and Holocaust denier. On the above-mentioned date, von Brunn entered the Holocaust Museum and produced a 0.22 caliber rifle, whereupon he shot and killed security officer Stephen Tyrone Johns. Von Brunn was immediately shot by two other officers before he could harm anyone else. Von Brunn died awaiting trial.[6]

The death of security officer Stephen Tyrone Johns is indeed a tragic loss. However, von Brunn's plan of committing mass murder at this religious and ideological site was not fully realized because the Holocaust Museum knew that it could be targeted by a deranged extremist and therefore had an array of security hardware and armed security officers posted at the entry way as well as other pertinent locations throughout the premises. They took the necessary precautions, as should any organization facing a risk because of the nature of their business.

ENDNOTES

[1] "Police Kill Discovery Building Gunman" http://www.nbcnews.com/id/38957020/ns/us_news-crime_and_courts/t/police-kill-discovery-building-gunman/#.VaACY2A9Xdk

[2] "LAX Shooting: LAPD Missed Intercepting Alleged Shooter by Minutes" http://www.latimes.com/local/lanow/la-me-ln-lax-shooting-lapd-missed-ciancia-20131104-story.html

[3] "Suspected LAX Gunman Had His Targets Clearly in Mind" http://www.latimes.com/local/la-me-1103-lax-shooting-20131103-story.html

[4] "Al Shabaab Calls for Attack on Mall of America in New Video" http://www.foxnews.com/world/2015/02/23/al-shabaab-reportedly-calls-for-attack-on-mall-america-in-new-video/

[5] "Suspect Is Seized in Capital in Threat at Federal Reserve" http://www.nytimes.com/1981/12/08/us/suspect-is-seized-in-capital-in-threat-at-federal-reserve.html?n=Top%2FReference%2FTimes%20Topics%2FSubjects%FH%2

[6] "At a Monument of Sorrow, A Burst of Deadly Violence" http://www.washingtonpost.com/wp-dyn/content/article/2009/06/10/AR2009061001768.html

Formulating a Plan and Putting it Into Action

CHAPTER 8

Seven Components of a Comprehensive Violence Prevention Plan

"In preparing for battle I have always found that plans are useless, but planning is indispensable."

—General Dwight D. Eisenhower

Contents

Abstract

Building an effective violence prevention program means planning for four main contingencies: violence prevention, threat management, violence response, and business recovery. To do this, an organization must develop each of the seven main components of the plan. Each is vitally important and all will fit into at least one of the four contingencies. The seven components are hiring processes, communication, policies, reporting processes, training, physical security, and the creation and implementation of a risk assessment and management team. Many organizations leave one or more of these critical aspects out of their plan and are blind-sided by the repercussions during and after an incident.

Keywords: business recovery; communication; physical security; risk assessment; threat management; violence prevention

The opening quote by General Eisenhower is apropos for this chapter. Plans frequently are unintentionally incomplete because you cannot anticipate every action and reaction that may occur or, as boxer Mike Tyson has been so eloquently quoted, "everyone has a plan till they get punched in the mouth." [1] However the planning process establishes goals, strategies and tactics. It trains you to think through problems with those goals in mind so that, as your plan evolves during the threat management process, you are always cognizant of both your desired results and those results that you want to avoid. When you have to adapt your plan to meet unanticipated challenges, there is always a risk that someone, usually an executive outside of the threat management process, will suggest or demand that a knee-jerk reaction be made that seemingly provides short-term satisfaction but actually escalates the threat. Knowing what your end game looks like will keep you on track and help you explain to the person applying the pressure why his or her proposed reaction may seem like a good idea but actually increases your organization's risk. Along with this explanation, you also need to be able to present your new tactics and articulate why they are the more prudent option.

THE SEVEN COMPONENTS OF A COMPREHENSIVE VIOLENCE PREVENTION PLAN

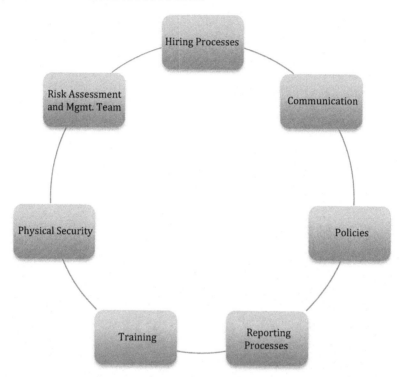

The Seven Components of a Comprehensive Violence Prevention Plan.

Creating a violence prevention program can seem like a daunting task and it can be as, in fact, you are actually planning for four contingencies. The first contingency plan is for the prevention of violence, the second contingency plan will prepare you to manage threats that are not thwarted by your prevention efforts, the third contingency plan is to prepare your response if violence occurs and the fourth contingency plan is to prepare for your recovery after an incident occurs. Fortunately the seven components of a comprehensive violence prevention plan will help you prepare for all four contingencies as shown in Table 8.1.

We will now take a closer look at the individual components of a comprehensive violence prevention plan.

Table 8.1 Four Contingencies

Violence prevention contingency	Threat management contingency	Violence response contingency	Business recovery contingency
• Hiring process • Communications • Policies • Processes • Training • Physical security	• Risk assessment and management team • Enhanced physical security	• Training • Risk assessment and management team • Physical security lockdown	• Training • Communications • Risk assessment and management team

Program Components to Prevent Violence
Hiring Processes

Most organizations do a very good job at determining and document-ing the requirements and qualities they are looking for in the candidates for their various jobs. However, some companies do not do a good job in determining and documenting the conduct and the reasons thereof that would disqualify a candidate for employment even if the candidate met the preferred requirements for education and prior experience. The first step in weeding out undesirable candidates is to also state in job descriptions or job postings what prior conduct will disqualify an applicant from being hired. Many organizations are reluctant to do this as it can be an uncomfortable process and requires legal reviews by your employment law attorneys whether they be in-house or outside contractors. In most instances there must be sound and specific reasons that have to be articulated and documented for listing disqualifying conduct. For example, if a children's daycare facility is hiring for any position that may come in contact with those in the care of the organization, a prior record of violence or sex-related crimes would be too great of a risk to grant employment. We recommend that a conviction for a crime of violence, including sexual assaults, be grounds for denying employment for any position. If the applicant is hired and later assaults someone on your premises, plaintiff's counsel will contend that their prior conviction made their future assault foreseeable and an example of your negligent hiring practices.

Questioning gaps in the employment record of applicants is one of the most important steps for the initial candidate screener. For example, in conducting a risk and vulnerability assessment for a client, we reviewed employment applications and found a current employee who had a two-year unexplained gap during her prior seven years with past employers. On questioning her, she admitted that this gap in employment time was because she had been incarcerated for two years for possession of illegal narcotics with the intent to distribute. Currently, social attitudes seem to be changing toward nonviolent offenders imprisoned for drug-related crimes and, if this woman was working in a janitorial capacity, her prison record might not have disqualified her for employment. However, the position she sought and obtained had her handing pharmaceuticals and controlled prescription narcotics for our client's organization. This unquestioned omission could cause many problems.

- If her criminal record was uncovered during a state or federal audit, the company could face fines and/or licensing revocations for negligent hiring practices.
- If she stole from the company, those losses could have been prevented by more detailed screening efforts.
- If shortages were found and her criminal records was subsequently uncovered during that investigation, she would become the focus of the investigation even though she might not have been involved.

- Further, the company's insurance carrier might deny their loss claim as the company failed to question the gap in employment or conduct a background check that would have uncovered her criminal record.

Anything on a candidate's resume or application that is not crystal clear needs to be questioned. Never assume that the issue is not important or that the candidate won't truthfully answer the question. Until the issue is pursued, you cannot judge its importance and many people will not lie under direct questioning. They may omit information, which they do not consider to be lying, but will answer truthfully when the questions are asked. Even if the applicant has lied about the issue, you have, at the very least, asked about the issue, the absence of which would increase the organization's potential liability should some incident occur at a later point in time. Any time that a candidate omits data or supplies questionable information, you must pursue the issue until information that puts the issue to rest is obtained. If this candidate is being seriously considered for the job, then an independent background check should also be conducted (we will discuss this further in another section).

Over our years in business, we have developed some screening questions that have been helpful in determining if someone has the potential to act out in anger or be a disruptive force in the workplace, such as:

- Tell me about a time when you had a disagreement with a coworker, supervisor, client, or customer. How did you handle the situation with this person? Is there anything that you would do differently if you were now faced with a similar situation?
- Tell us about a conflict that you handled well.
- Tell us about a conflict that you did not handle well.
- Tell us about the best manager or supervisor you ever worked for and describe what he or she did to earn such high regard.
- Tell us about the worst manager or supervisor you ever worked for and describe what he or she did to become your worst boss. Do you have any other examples? (Note: If the candidate seems to only have worked for "bad bosses" in the past, then the candidate is probably not going to get along with your managers and supervisors any better than with prior employers.)
- Is there any reason why a past employer might tell us that you separated from that company for reasons different than the ones you listed on your application? For example, you stated that you left most of your prior employers because of "personal reasons" or because you received a better job offer. Is there any reason why any of these companies might tell

us that you were fired? (This is especially important to ask if there is a sizable gap in time between employment with two companies indicative that the candidate's departure from employer A was not planned and there was not a standing offer from company B that precipitated the job change. Over the course of our experience, we have heard some tall tales in response to this question usually involving more bad bosses.)

These questions should not be asked consecutively but sprinkled throughout the other applicant inquiries that you normally ask. Also, these questions should be vetted with your employment law attorneys before they are added to your screening repertoire. You want to make sure the questions are legal to ask in the state in which your facility is located. *Note: Make sure the legality of the questions is answered rather than an attorney or other executive merely passing judgment on their perceived effectiveness of the questions.* Frequently an attorney or perhaps a human resource executive will not realize the importance of these questions, feeling that no applicants would supply negative information about themselves during an interview. To some sense they are correct; no rational person would supply an abundance of damaging information about him- or herself, but these questions are not designed to identify rational candidates. They are designed to identify the irrational person who felt justified in reacting to a situation with anger and/or other forms of workplace disruption of which the person enjoys retelling the stories.

Once the candidate pool has been narrowed to a final applicant, it is time to conduct further screening via a drug test and background check. You will recall that substance abuse is one of the warning signs that an employee is having trouble that, at the very least, will result in reliability and job performance issues and, in the worst-case scenario, might escalate to disruptive and even violent behavior. If any of your facilities reside in an area where recreational marijuana has been decriminalized, your organization needs to legally determine and document how recreational use will affect your hiring standards. For example, if you are hiring for a position that operates dangerous machinery, then any indication of impairment or substance addiction may be too great of a risk for employment.

Criminal background checks should be conducted within the applicant's county and state of residence as well as all counties and states in which they resided for the last seven years. Seven years is the cutoff parameter given, as most jurisdictions will not provide any earlier information. You should consider running a nationwide check as well to see if the candidate has omitted any prior residences. Recently we conducted a background check on a subject whose personnel data showed that he lived in Michigan and Florida. No offenses were listed in either of those states, however a nationwide check showed someone with the same name who had a criminal record in the state of New York. On drilling down further into New York's data, we found two burglary convictions belonging to someone with the same name, date of birth, and social security number, in other words, a direct match. Failure to conduct a nationwide search would not have uncovered this information.

Drug tests and background checks can be expensive and take time that you probably would rather not spend. You will, however, want to make sure that jobs that increase the potential for exposure and risk to the company have additional steps of vetting. If you are hiring a telemarketer, then any future misconduct might not put your organization at an enhanced level of exposure. However, if you are hiring a driver who will be transporting highly flammable, explosive, and/or toxic chemicals, you cannot risk even the perception of negligent hiring and will want to make sure that his or her driving history is good and that the driver is not using intoxicants and/or illegal drugs that may impair his or her driving abilities. You will also want to make sure that there is nothing in the driver's background indicating that he or she employed violence as a form of vengeance in the past. If so, the driver's access to dangerous chemicals again puts your organization at risk.

Communications

There are several components to your communication plan. The first component is how to communicate that the organization in putting together a violence prevention plan without causing undue concern. We have found that the best method is to align the violence prevention plan with your organization's core values. Usually one of the core values relates to the well-being and/or safety of the company's employees. Announcing that your violence prevention plan is an offshoot of a wellness program or safety core value is a great way to initiate the communication process. You can also relate that school systems have already adopted similar plans with which your employees are already familiar (if they have children). Failure to announce the reasons behind the establishment of your violence prevention plan will cause your associates to determine them on their own, the most popular of which is "there must be some problem that the company is not telling us about." Early and honest communication will prevent the rumor mill from unleashing false and/or disturbing information.

The second component of your communication plan is to determine how to keep the violence prevention plan flourishing after it has been introduced. Every employee in every organization has sat through a program introduction that will fade from everyone's memory in a few weeks or months. For this reason, we prefer to avoid referring to your violence prevention plan as a *program*. Programs are temporary and your associates recognize that *program* is a code word indicating a project that will shortly be out of sight and out of mind. This is why we prefer that the plan be introduced as a component of a core value that is recognized to be a long-term company strategy.

Once the violence prevention plan has been introduced and the initial training has been completed, there are a variety of ways to keep the information fresh in the minds of your associates:

- *Ongoing training.* We recommend to our clients that ongoing training occur at least every other year. The content can be a refresher on the fundamental components of the initial training, any components you have found that need to be reinforced, and the discussion of workplace-related violence that has recently been profiled in the news media. This discussion would include highlighting how your plan would have prevented these incidents as well as the introduction of any changes or new components to your plan that have been added after a thorough review of the incidents reported in the media.

- *Reminder posters.* Posters that provide fundamental information from your plan can be placed around the premises in locations that you determine to be appropriate. To be effective, the information, format, and color scheme should be changed quarterly. If you leave them up longer, they just become wallpaper.

- *Reminder messages to be implanted into the material used during departmental or group meetings.* This information must be a short two- to three-minute discussion regarding a component of the plan that needs to be reinforced. If you make it a longer message, you run the risk of it being cut if the meeting is running long. Additionally, the explanation of a short concept is easily remembered. Longer discussions tax the memory of the audience as they cannot remember all of the different topics presented during the department meeting. Make yours short and impactful so it will be fresh in their minds.

The third and fourth component of your communications plan occurs if a violent incident happens; your communication challenge then becomes how to communicate with your associates and the public. The short answer is *with honesty and sensitivity.* The longer answer will be covered in Chapter 12 *Managing the Aftermath of Violence.*

Policies

The first issue we want to discuss is to dismiss the notion of having zero tolerance policies. Zero tolerance policies are a bad idea for several reasons. Occupational Safety professionals, as well as the Occupational Safety and Health Administration (OSHA), have long recognized that zero tolerance policies encourage the underreporting of incidents. Managers and supervisors look at zero tolerance policies and feel that *zero* incidents is the standard to which their performance will be measured. Therefore they are concerned that if an incident occurs, it will be considered a black mark on their managerial performance. So, instead of reporting disturbing behavior or threats to the personnel within the organization who are trained to investigate and assess them, the managers either ignore the threats and disruptive behavior or attempt to handle them by themselves. Neither of those two options is acceptable. Ignoring disturbing behavior allows it to escalate, and when untrained personnel attempt to handle threats and disturbing behavior on their own, their actions are typically incomplete or they respond in a manner that escalates the risk toward the organization and their associates.

Another reason that zero tolerance policies are a bad idea is that they tend to lure organizations into dispensing punishments that do not fit the crime. For example, there have been media reports of schools suspending students and considering expulsions after noting a box cutter in a student's vehicle's cup holder that was issued to the student at the grocery store where the student worked after school. [2] In another incident a female honor student was suspended and faced expulsion after school officials noticed plastic rifles in the back of her vehicle that were used by the military drill team in which she participated. [3] These students were suspended and faced expulsion, meaning that they would have to finish school via an online program, would not be allowed to attend or participate in any school functions, and would not be allowed to participate in the school's graduation ceremony. Fortunately these incidents were brought to the attention of the news media, and the subsequent outcry from the public caused the schools to decrease the suspension time and cease the expulsion process. As we mentioned, the proposed punishments did not fit the crimes. Should a student be disciplined for having a box cutter in his or her vehicle? If it violates a known school policy, then the answer is "yes." Should the student have his or her teenaged life ruined by expulsion and having to find an alternative method for completing his or her education? Absolutely not!

Another reason that zero tolerance policies are a bad idea is that they can cause an organization to shortcut the investigation and assessment process. As any violation of the zero tolerance policy results in the accused's termination, some organizations do not see the need to investigate and assess the violation, as the outcome is predetermined. This is a poor course of action, as an investigation might prove that the accused is innocent or the investigation might also uncover that the violator of the policy poses a serious threat to the organization that requires further action to be taken to safeguard the people and premises. All of these problems can emanate from a policy that predetermines terminations and undervalues the investigation and assessment process.

While we do not recommend zero tolerance policies to our clients there are six other policies we recommend that organizations should have and enforce:

1. *A policy that defines weapons and prohibits their possession on the organization's premises.* The definition would include firearms, knives, chemical sprays, impact weapons, or other implements that could cause injury or death and are not necessary or issued for the performance of the employee's job function. The company's premises should be defined within the confines of state law. Some states allow companies to ban weapons

from their buildings, grounds, and parking facilities, including employee vehicles, while other states do not allow employers to prohibit firearms that are locked in an employee's vehicle. The policy should apply to employees who are conducting company business off premises, such as performing their job duties at a client's site, and also apply at company-sponsored events that occur off of the company's recognized premises, such as a company picnic held at a park or a company Christmas party at a hotel or restaurant.

2. *A policy that defines and prohibits inappropriate behavior*, such as: making offensive or degrading remarks or conduct, engaging in any type of harassment or discrimination, possessing or using illegal substances, engaging in an act of violence, and engaging in intimidating behavior such as:

   - Taunting and malicious teasing
   - Making threatening remarks or engaging in threatening physical behavior
   - Creating a hostile work environment
   - Stalking

   In other words, your policy on inappropriate behavior should mirror OSHA's definition of workplace violence which, as you recall from Chapter 1, is "Workplace violence is *any act* or *threat* of physical violence, *harassment, intimidation*, or *other threatening disruptive behavior* that occurs at the work site. It ranges from threats and *verbal abuse* to physical assaults and even homicide." (emphasis added)

3. *A policy that requires employees to report restraining orders that cover the workplace and encourages employees to report all restraining orders, threats, disturbing behavior, and breaches of security protocols.* You can't maintain the security of the premises if you do not know the risks that are threatening your organization.

4. *A policy that requires managers and supervisors to immediately report issues to the appropriate designees or departments* when they are notified of restraining orders, threats, disturbing behavior, and breach of security protocols.

5. *A policy that prohibits employees from talking to the news media* and instructs them to forward all media inquiries to the media relation's designee.

6. *A policy that prohibits employees from posting or otherwise entering into discussion about company business on social media sites.*

Reporting Processes

To encourage employees to report threats, disturbing behavior, restraining orders, and breaches of security protocols, you need to provide a vehicle that facilitates this process. Traditionally this has been accomplished by a direct, one-on-one discussion between the concerned employee and the employee's manager or supervisor. It was soon found that some people do not feel comfortable coming forward and stating their concerns in a face-to-face meeting. This led to the rise of anonymous phone services that will transcribe the employee's concerns and forward them to the appropriate management designee. However, the generation that is newly entering the workforce prefers to communicate through technology rather than the telephone. This necessitates that businesses respond by developing new processes whereby employees can anonymously report concerns via private forum messages, email, text message, or an online form. Along with increasing the probability that concerns will be reported, there is another upside to this type of communication: If the reported concern does not contain enough information to initiate an investigation, your technology solution can be built in a manner that allows you to respond to the anonymous respondent and request further information.

Staff and Management Training
This topic will be covered in Chapter 9.

The Situational Assessment and Management Team
This topic will be covered in Chapter 10.

Physical Security
Your physical security plan has many missions:
- To protect guests and personnel
- To keep people who do not belong in your building out of your building
- To keep unauthorized personnel or guests from being able to access sensitive areas within the building
- To protect confidential information
- To protect hazardous materials used by your business

The first step is to conduct a physical security assessment. Here are some of the things you need to identify:
- Are there any job functions or physical locations within the facility that run a higher risk of being victimized by violence? If so, what will you do to enhance the safety for those job functions or locations?
- Are there any types of visitors who pose a higher risk of violence? If so, what will you do to identify those visitors and how will you enhance security when they are present?
- Identify sensitive areas and review enhancements to provide appropriate security. Some areas of sensitivity are, but may not be limited to:
  - Server rooms.
  - Areas where confidential information is stored.
  - Areas where money or valuable items are stored.
  - Areas containing flammable or explosive materials, which might include the storage areas for propane-powered floor-cleaning equipment and areas where gasoline and fertilizers for lawn care are stowed.
  - Areas within research and medical facilities where dangerous chemicals and radioactive material is kept.
  - Shipping and receiving areas. Shipping and receiving areas frequently do not get the same levels of security that higher traffic areas within a facility receive. This is a bad idea as these are prime areas for theft. Additionally if a view is taken that a breach of security is improbable within an area, that area is then vulnerable and becomes a more likely target. Several years ago a colleague related an incident that occurred

when a woman who perceived that the organization's environmental programs were subpar was harassing the CEO. One day the woman telephoned the CEO's office to state that she was in town and on her way to see him. My colleague and her security team rushed to the lobby to detain and remove the woman from their premises. After several minutes, the CEO phoned the lobby to tell the security team that the intruder was in his office. During detention, the intruder stated that as she was walking down the street toward the lobby she passed an alley where the shipping and receiving area was located. She walked through the area and was not challenged. Further, there was no access control on the freight elevator, which is how she gained access to the top floor of the high-rise building. Those lapses in security were quickly corrected but clearly show how an area deemed unlikely to need security became vulnerable.

- Three important components of your physical security plan are your alarm system, your access control system, and your closed circuit television system. As these types of systems are frequently upgraded, we are not going to recommend any equipment or features as our recommendations will likely be outdated by the time you purchase the book. We recommend that you work with a trusted security systems integrator to review the needs of your facility and its sensitive areas and show you different hardware and software solutions to consider.

- There are other important components to your physical security plan that should be reviewed:

  - Is the exterior lighting bright enough to illuminate anyone in the area and does it allow victims, witnesses, and your closed circuit television system to obtain a good look at any intruder?

  - Do you have emergency buttons located throughout your building and parking facility? These mechanisms should have an intercom feature that would allow the person activating the system to speak with an operator to communicate the nature of the emergency (e.g. injury, medical issue, criminal activity, etc.).

  - Do you have safe rooms where associates can secure themselves in the event of a rampage shooter?

  - Can you lock down your facility with the press of a button? This is possible and extremely important. We were once called in to consult for a distribution center after an incident had occurred. The husband of an employee called stating that he was on the way to kill his wife and her supervisor with whom he incorrectly perceived to be having an affair with his wife. The manager immediately called the police and initiated a lockdown of the building. They had never practiced an emergency lockdown before and, as this was a distribution center, there were more than 40 doors that needed to be secured. The managers, supervisors, and security guard were running to lock the doors and began with the doors in the back of the building because those were the highest traffic locations. All of the employees entered through the back doors, as did the drivers making deliveries and pickups from the distribution center. The enraged husband, however, was not an employee and the only way he knew to enter the building was through the front lobby entrance and this is where the first arriving police officer shot him dead when he did not drop the shotgun he was pointing at the officer. When you need to lock down a facility, you need to do it quickly and you need to be able to lock them down via one control mechanism.

To arm or not to arm

We are frequently asked to provide an opinion as to whether a particular business should have armed or unarmed security. We touched on this in the previous chapter and our guidance is fairly straightforward. If, by the very nature of your organization, you are a potential target for hate groups or terrorist organizations, then you should have a qualified, professional armed security staff. If not, then you need to be cognizant of times when potential threats are present and bring in armed professionals until said threat has dissipated.

Now that you are familiar with the components of a violence prevention plan as well as the factors that necessitate those components, let's review another case study and apply what has been presented.

Alton Alexander Nolan was a risky hire in the first place. In January 2011, he was convicted of multiple felony drug charges, assault and battery of a police officer, and escape from detention. On release from incarceration in March 2013, Vaughn Foods in Moore, Oklahoma, hired Nolan. Vaughn Foods is a wholesaler of fresh and processed produce.

Nolan was known to engage in verbal confrontations with coworkers and supervisors for which he had been suspended in the past. On September 25, 2014, Nolan was summoned to the human resource office, located in a different building from where he worked. On arrival, he found that he was being suspended for a verbal confrontation with a supervisor, whereupon he told her that he "did not like white people" and Nolan stormed out of the human resource office, got into his vehicle, and drove off. One of the human resource associates notified Mark Vaughn, the chief operating officer, of Nolan's outrage.

A short time later Nolan crashed into a parked car at the main warehouse. With a knife that he had retrieved during his departure, he slit the throat of the first person he encountered at the warehouse, 54-year-old Colleen Hulford, and then beheaded her. After that he turned his attention toward 43-year-old Traci Johnson, slashing her throat and face but was killed when Vaughn, who was a reserve deputy sheriff, shot him with a rifle. The shooting of Nolan undoubtedly saved Johnson's life [4, 5, 6].

Alton Nolen's case has not yet come to trial and until then, the pertinent facts of the investigation will not be revealed. As such, we do not wish to make any assumptions about what Vaughn Foods did or did not have in terms of a violence prevention plan because none of that information is available at the time of our writing. In not wishing to cast unwarranted aspersions, we will simply ask if certain components of the violence prevention plan as previously outlined could have been of help in this instance, such as:

- A policy that excludes violent offenders from employment
- A criminal background check
- Drug testing
- A thorough assessment of Nolan's behavior and assessment of his potential for violence
- Access control, including the ability to quickly lock down the campus, to have kept Nolan out after his suspension
- Employee training on how to respond to a violent attack
- A security plan on how to respond if Nolan returned to the campus

Again, we do not know whether Vaughn Foods had any of these components in place; we do not know the extent of training and drilling had that taken place prior to the incident; and we do not know the level of execution of any components during the incident. We are merely asking the reader to take the violence prevention plan presented in this chapter and apply them to the facts as described in the preceding box.

ENDNOTES

[1] Mike Tyson Quote http://www.brainyquote.com/quotes/quotes/m/miketyson382439 .html
[2] "Blaine Student Suspended over Box Cutter in the Car," *Winona Daily News*, September 18, 2008 http://www.winonadailynews.com/news/blaine-student-suspended-over-box -cutter-in-car/article_52a399c2-cfdb-5945-ab50-4576cfc5807d.html

[3] "Teen Marine Honor Student Suspended for Prop Gun (for Drills)," WorldNet Daily, February 11, 2009 http://www.760kfmb.com/story/9834420/teen-marine-honor-student-suspended-for-prop-gun-for-drills?clienttype=printable

[4] Sebastian Murdock, "Alton Nolan Allegedly Beheads Oklahoma Coworker After Firing," *Huffington Post*, September 26, 2014 http://www.huffingtonpost.com/2014/09/26/alton-nolan-beheads-cowor_n_5888500.html

[5] Sean Murphy, "Oklahoma Man Charged with Murder in Beheading," Associated Press, September 30, 2014 http://news.yahoo.com/oklahoma-man-charged-murder-beheading-154028051.html

[6] Abby Ohlheiser, "What We Know about Anton Nolen, Who Has Been Charged with Murder in the Oklahoma Beheading Case," *Washington Post* http://www.washingtonpost.com/news/post-nation/wp/2014/09/30/what-we-know-about-alton-nolen-who-has-been-charged-with-murder-in-the-oklahoma-beheading-case/

CHAPTER 9

Staff and Management Training

"In the time of crisis, people don't rise to the occasion they revert to their level of training"

—Anonymous

Contents

Abstract

As a general rule, people who find themselves in a serious life and death crisis situation do not rise to the challenge, perform heroically, and have clarity of thought. Most people fall prey to their human reactions of fear, panic, or denial, unless they have received proper training. Those who do generally will default to that training. It is for this reason that training at all levels must occur. Training for the general employee population must include six vital components, which will explain (1) why the training is being conducted, (2) the real risks employees face, (3) what is already in place to protect them, (4) their role in protecting the premises, (5) how to react if violence occurs, and (6) what to expect in the aftermath. Training will emphasize the fact that in many instances of severe workplace violence, employees or others in a location can and often have, fought back and survived, if not defeated the attacker. Creating a victor's mindset among your employees is key to creating a feeling of informed empowerment rather than that of helpless victim. Managers play a key role in ensuring they remain aware of the warning signs of potential violence and that they understand their role as reporters to the team designated to assess and manage the threat.

Keywords: fight; hide; management training; physical security; run; safe rooms; staff training; victor's mindset e violence prevention program.

Photo credit: Pavel L Photo and Video / Shutterstock.com

We don't know who coined chapter opening quote (and we paraphrased it), but situational reactions to violence certainly prove it to be true. Lt. Col. David Grossman points out in his lectures that deaths caused by school fires are nearly nonexistent since the advent of fire drills and fire technology that began in the early 1960s. Regardless of what building you are in, if a fire alarm is activated, everyone knows what to do and they do it without thinking, because it has become an automatic response. This came about through decades of training and drilling. Unfortunately, the same cannot be said about how people react when gunfire rings out.

In our experience we have seen people exhibit two reactions to gunfire if they have not trained and drilled on how to respond. The first reaction is denial. In some instances people deny that what they heard was gunfire and stayed where they were, putting themselves in danger of becoming the next fatality. In reviewing building security camera video of shooting events, we have also seen people react by heading toward the sound of the gunfire to see what happened when they should be heading away from the danger instead of toward it.

The other reaction that we frequently see is panic so severe that it prohibits rational thought and action. In our experience panic usually manifests itself in two forms: (1) frantic agitation and (2) becoming frozen in fear.

Neither of these reactions is optimal for survival when a rampage shooter has invaded the premises. Those reacting in frantic agitation, such as running about but not sure where to go and yelling for help or shouting unnecessary questions, are a detriment to their survival and the survival of those who are with them. They can draw more attention to their area thereby increasing the chances that the rampage shooter will head their way and they can impede the actions of those who actually do know what should be done in this time of crisis.

The way to circumvent denial and panic is through training and drilling.

ASSOCIATE TRAINING PLAN

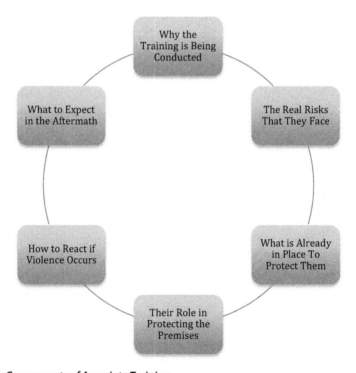

The Six Components of Associate Training.

The first component to the training is to explain why your organization has decided to conduct violence prevention training. Do not be anxious about this; they all know of workplace homicides from the news media and will be glad that your organization is finally addressing this topic. As we mentioned earlier, tying your violence prevention plan to an existing core value or long-term strategic imperative is an excellent way to explain your rationale for the plan. Whether it is linked to employee wellness or employee safety initiatives, it will be well received. You will also need to explain why the training is necessary. Grossman's references to fire drills are perhaps the best and most common sense explanation you will find. You want to build the same automatic reactions to gunfire as there is to a fire alarm.

The next step is to define workplace violence and, again, our guidance is to use the definition from the Occupational Safety and Health Administration: "Workplace violence is any act or threat of physical violence, harassment, intimidation, or other threatening disruptive behavior that occurs at the work site. It ranges from threats and verbal abuse to physical assaults and even homicide." OSHA definition of workplace violence https://www.osha.gov/SLTC/workplaceviolence/.

After defining workplace violence, it is then time to explain the real risks that they face in your business environment. Of the three primary risks–relationship violence, associate violence, and external violence – the risks that most organizations will be faced with is relationship violence and associate violence. Most organizations are not centers of government and finance nor do they have the symbolic and ideological significance that will attract hate groups, lone wolf killers, or terrorist cells. All three primary risks should be discussed, but it should be done so in the context of the most likely risks that the organization will face.

The next phase of the training is to present what is already in place to protect them. This is where you will discuss your current state of physical security, such as closed-circuit television systems, security guards, alarm systems, access control, and so forth. This is also where you will discuss the policies you have in place related to violence prevention and why you have them. These can be any of the policies outlined in the prior chapter, such as your company's weapons policy and the policy on inappropriate behavior, as well as policies requiring that only one person at a time enters through an access-controlled area, policies related to the reporting of threats, and restraining orders and any other policy related to the safety and security of your workforce.

This is also the point to discuss the addition of new policies and other enhancements to increase their protection while in your care. Such things might include new access control systems, new policies, the placement of emergency call boxes throughout the building and parking facility, and the introduction of safe rooms and periodic lockdown drills. Lockdown drills are extremely important in getting your associates out of denial and panic and into the survival mode.

Safe rooms and lockdown drills are becoming more common in businesses and many public buildings. Safe rooms should be an enclosure, lockable from the inside, preferably with no windows or at least no interior windows that allow someone in the hallway to see into the room. Even if the enclosures in the facility all have interior windows, there are film coatings available that are bullet and shatter resistant and have a frosted or clouded texture that make it difficult to tell if people are inside, especially if they are lying on the floor. If you cannot afford to put the film on all of the enclosures, then have it applied to enough of the rooms in different areas so that everyone has access to a safe room. In most instances of prior rampage shootings, the killer, who is looking for a large body count, typically bypasses locked doors. Shooters know they have a finite amount of time before armed first responders arrive (usually 12 to 15 minutes) and they want to increase their body count rather than waste time trying to gain access to a locked room.

Lockdown drills should be conducted at least twice a year. There are different ways to execute the drill. We recommend that the drill event be announced about a week in advance. You do not have to provide the exact date and time, but it is a good idea to give people some notice so that they are not overcome with anxiety when the lockdown alert is given. Some companies begin the drill by firing a starter or blank firing pistol to provide the most realistic scenario possible. Other companies ring some type of alarm that is easily differentiated from their fire or severe weather alarms, while still other organizations have two preprogrammed intercom announcements that can be played at the push of a button. The first announcement is for drills and states, "This is a lockdown drill. Please execute all lockdown procedures at once." This announcement is usually given three times and followed by an all clear message once the drill has been completed. The situational risk assessment and management team should monitor the drills and be looking for a quick acknowledgment of the alert with everyone getting into a safe room as fast as possible. If the response was poor and slow, then be honest with the associate and schedule a follow-up drill within the next two weeks. Ask for associate feedback, as they may have experienced problems with the lockdown plan that the situational risk assessment team did not anticipate when the plan was constructed. Don't worry that the plan wasn't perfect. Part of the reason for conducting the drill is to identify weaknesses and correct them before the real thing happens.

The second preprogrammed lockdown announcement is used in the event of an actual violent incident and states, "This building is now in lockdown and this is not a drill. Please execute all lockdown procedures at once. Police and emergency responders are on their way." Again this announcement is repeated at least three times. Part of this announcement is intended for the shooter. "Please execute lockdown procedures" may cause confusion or anxiety for the shooter as he or she doesn't know what that means and hopefully construes it to mean that the associates are about to take defensive actions. "Police and emergency responders are on their way to the building" is designed to let the shooter know that armed help is on the way and the shooter had better be leaving.

The fourth component and an extremely important one is the role that your associates play in the safety and security of your organization. You will want to outline the issues that you want reported to management starting with the warning signs detailed in Chapter 6, which are:

- Someone seeking revenge
- Someone who has withdrawn from social connections
- Someone who has exhibited negative changes in appearance and hygiene
- Someone who believes the organization or some associates within the organization are responsible for all of his or her problems
- Someone exhibiting signs of addiction
- Someone who is easily angered
- Someone who is communicating violent and/or suicidal ideation
- Someone who is communicating contextually inappropriate interest in firearms and explosives and indicates a recent acquisition of multiple weapons
- Someone who demonstrates contextually inappropriate fascination of prior acts of mass violence
- Someone who has become recklessness with his or her personal life with no regard to the potential consequences
- Someone who has either communicated about or directed people toward his or her manifesto

Note: It is important to reinforce three explanatory points during the training:
1. You are looking for recent and sustained changes in someone's normal behavior rather than someone who is just having a bad day.
2. Any behavior that an associate finds disturbing should be reported even if it is different from the points listed earlier.
3. The goal of your violence prevention plan is to intervene and get the subject the help he or she needs before anyone gets hurt.

There are also other things that should be reported:

- Suspicious persons, such as people who have no apparent business in the facility but are hanging around, observing the routine of the building, perhaps even taking photographs or making diagrams
- Suspicious conditions or breaches of security protocols, such as a door that has always been locked which is now being blocked open
- Threats
- Restraining orders
- Disturbing behavior
- Issues where an associate is the victim of unwanted attention by another associate or outsider

Note that it is particularly important to impress upon your associates that your ability to protect them is extremely hampered if they do not tell you what suspicions they have, the disturbing behavior they have witnessed, or the threats that they or someone else has received. It should also be explained that they should not merely assume that a manager or supervisor will see the same things they have observed as people exhibiting disturbing behavior frequently cease that behavior when in the presence of a manager or supervisor.

This training phase should also include whom to notify of their concerns, usually a manager or human resource representative. As mentioned in Chapter 8, you also need to have a reporting option for those who wish to remain anonymous and those options for protecting anonymity should also be explained.

The next phase of associate training is how to react if violence occurs. The conventional wisdom recommended by the Federal Bureau of Investigation and the Department of Homeland Security is to:

- Run if you can.
- Hide if you can't.
- Fight back if you must.

If there is shooting inside of a building and your associates can safely find their way to an exit, then they should run, escape, get to a safe location and call the police. They should give the police the address of the building where the shooting is occurring and give them as much information about the shooter(s) as they know, such as how many are there, what they look like and what they are wearing, what part of the building were they in, and so forth. They should also tell the police where they, themselves are and provide their physical description, including a description of the clothes they are wearing and an accounting of how many other associates may be with them.

If they cannot escape, then they should get to a safe room, lock the door, turn off the lights, and lie down. They should also silence any noise-making devices, such as cell phones, tablet computers, laptops, and so forth. If safe to do so, they should call the police and give them the same information as previously mentioned:

- Location of the shooting
- Current location of the shooters, if known
- Description of the shooters
- Their location within the building
- How many people are with them
- Is anybody injured and if the injury is life-threatening
- Description of the associates

If they cannot get to a safe room, then they should hide anywhere they can, such as under a desk or inside of a closet and remember that silence is their friend – so they should turn off cell phones as well as any other noise making devices. Hiding might also entail playing dead. Once the police arrive in sufficient numbers to enter the building, the event will be over fairly quickly, but those who are in lockdown or hiding should wait until the police inform them that it is safe to emerge.

It is important for everyone to understand that they can successfully defend themselves from an attacker, including an active shooter. There is even research that has been done on this subject. Texas State University released a study in March 2013 that examined 84 active shooting events between 2000 and 2010. [1] In these 84 shooting events, the intended victims fought back in 16 of the incidents. In all 16 events, the intended victims were able to subdue and disarm the shooter. In only 3 of the events were the intended victims armed, in the other 13 they did not possess firearms. Let's briefly examine some other situations in which the victims were victorious. You may be familiar with some of these incidents:

- On December 7, 1983, Colin Ferguson boarded an afternoon rush hour commuter train running between New York City and Long Island. He was intent on killing a large number of people, but "out of respect to Mayor David Dinkins" he did not begin his massacre until the train passed New York City's boundaries. He opened fire on the commuters with a 9 mm pistol, killing six people and wounding 19 before passengers tackled and disarmed him while he was trying to reload the pistol for the second time. [2]

- October 30, 1994, 26-year-old Francisco Martin Duran traveled from Colorado to Washington, D.C., and, as horrified tourists looked on, began shooting at the White House with a Chinese SKS semiautomatic carbine. Approximately 20 rounds of ammunition hit the White House but did not penetrate the bullet-resistant glass or walls of the structure. While attempting to reload the carbine, at least two passers-by wrestled him to the Pennsylvania Avenue sidewalk before uniformed Secret Service agents took him into custody. [3]

- On September 11, 2001, terrorists boarded four commercial flights and hijacked the planes. Two of them were flown into the World Trade towers in New York City and one was flown into the Pentagon in Washington, D.C. The passengers of United Flight 93, the last of the hijacked planes, had called friends and emergency agencies and learned that their fate was to die as their plane was crashed into some symbolic and highly populated building as had occurred with the other three flights. The passengers realized that it was too late to save themselves, but they were determined not to allow the terrorists to complete their mission. They fought back and forced the terrorists to crash the plane in a wooded area in Pennsylvania, denying them the ability to kill anyone on the ground. The passengers on the first three flights are commonly referred to as "victims" while the passengers on Flight 93 are always referred to as "heros."

- On December 20, 2010, 25-year-old Jared Lee Loughner posted on his social media page: "I have this huge goal at the end of my life: 165 rounds fired in a minute!" On Saturday, January 8, 2011, he stepped up to the front of a crowd where Congresswoman Gabby Giffords was meeting constituents beside an Arizona grocery store. He then opened up with a pistol and killed six people and injured 13, including Giffords before crowd members subdued and disarmed him while he was trying to reload. [4]

- On November 25, 2013, 19-year-old Trevonnte Brown boarded a Seattle bus and began robbing people of their cell phones at gunpoint. After successfully robbing several riders, he encountered a passenger who did not want to comply. This passenger grabbed the front of Brown's pistol with his left hand and pushed the muzzle back toward the Brown. The passenger then leapt up and began pummeling Brown with his right hand. At that point some of the passengers jumped on Brown and subdued him until the police arrived a few minutes later. [5]

From the aforementioned incidents, as well as many others, we see four tactics that are commonly repeated:
1. Having a victor's mindset
2. Taking advantage of an opening
3. Applying force in numbers
4. The psychological advantage of the victim

The victor's mindset is present in every situation where the victims overpower the shooter. The mindset is simply a realization that no one has the right to take your life and a commitment that if someone tries to take it they will be met with a relentless counterattack that the shooter is not prepared to meet. In the Long Island railroad massacre, the White House shooter, United Flight 93, and the shooting of Congresswoman Gabby Giffords, those who fought back did not have that mindset at the beginning of the incident but developed it during the attack. In the Seattle bus robbery, the last intended victim already had the mindset as he fought back immediately and decisively.

During the Long Island railroad massacre, the White House shooting, and the Gabby Giffords shooting, the victims used the moments when the shooters were reloading as an opening to launch their counterattack. An opening is simply any moment where the shooter is not focused on the victims or any moment when the shooter is distracted from shooting, such as when the firearm has been shot dry and needs reloading. However, rather than waiting for a shooter to reload, you can create an opening that allows you to commence your counterattack. Throwing something into the face of an attacker is a great distraction. When something is thrown into someone's face, there are naturally occurring responses that he or she cannot control, such as head ducking, head tilting back, eyes inadvertently closing, hands coming up to block the incoming missile from the face. Those openings are brief but not difficult to create. Throwing a briefcase, laptop or tablet computer, pen, or even the half-eaten muffin on your desk can provide the opening you need. A great implement to keep in mind is the fire extinguisher. If you are inside any office building, retail shop, school, manufacturing facility, distribution center, or other building, fire extinguishers abound. A blast in the face from the extinguisher can create the opening you need and the canister can be used to launch your counterattack. Common objects found within the environment where the attack occurs can also be used as weapons to help overcome the attacker. A high school student's backpack is a formidable impact weapon when swung or launched at an attacker. A large pair of office scissors or ballpoint pens can be used as effective stabbing implements.

One of the factors present in all of the incidents cited is the fact that force in numbers can overwhelm an attacker. It is also noted that in most instances, once a person makes the decision to counterattack, others quickly join in. In the Seattle bus robbery one passenger who had been robbed was trailing the robber through the bus when the final victim launched his counterattack. The trailing passenger and another passenger leapt in almost immediately and assisted in subduing and disarming the robber. In the shooting at the White House, one tourist tackled the shooter and another was close behind. It is obvious that the clearheaded action of one person during a crisis influences the actions of others.

Victims may not realize it, but in many cases, they have a distinct psychological advantage over the attacker. As discussed in earlier chapters, although many shooting attacks seem to be impromptu actions, they are not. After a mass homicide, investigators typically find a sufficient amount of evidence to show that an inordinate amount of preparation went into the attack and the shooter spent many months planning the event.

All of this planning contributes to factors giving a psychological advantage to the victims, which is simply this: The attacker does not expect resistance. The meticulous planning that the attacker has done has also produced a movie of this event that plays continuously in the attacker's mind, which the attacker has watched thousands of times. When the part plays showing the attacker walking into the room with his or her firearm, all the attacker sees are cowering, compliant victims. The attacker is not prepared for resistance because that scene is not in the mental movie he or she has been watching over and over. Therefore, when someone blasts the attacker with a fire extinguisher and smacks the attacker with the red canister, the attacker is not prepared to react and his or her attack may fall apart, especially if force in numbers is then applied. Remember Mike Tyson's quote from Chapter 8: "Everyone has a plan till they get punched in the mouth."

We are certainly not saying that unarmed associates should set out to actively engage a shooter with a firearm. But if cornered and the only alternative is to die, then adopt the victor's mindset, find common objects to use as weapons, and take advantage of the force you have in the numbers that are with you.

The last phase of the associate training is to inform them of what will happen in the aftermath of an incident. They need to understand that when the police arrive, their primary objective is to neutralize the shooter(s). Evacuating the innocent and tending to the injured are secondary to putting an end to the shooting. As such, they will probably not stop to talk to anyone as they enter the building. If they do, it will be to ask questions and they will be looking for quick and concise answers. Your associates will also be treated as suspects until the police have ensured that all shooters have been identified and killed or in custody. Therefore your employees should expect to be detained by the police, possibly have officers point guns at them, handcuff them, search them, and place them on the ground. They should understand that this is temporary and they will be released just as soon as the police have cleared the building and have an understanding of what occurred.

Your employees should also expect that the new media will arrive and will want to talk to them. They need to understand that your organization has a policy that prohibits them from talking to the reporters and they need to understand why. At the point that the news media arrives, your employees do not know the whole story of what happened and they do not want to supply conjecture or assumptions that can impede or jeopardize the police investigation. Their best course of action is to simply say, "No comment."

Social media also plays a new role in providing misinformation to the public, and your employees should be prohibited from discussing company issues on social media for the exact same reasons that they should not talk to the news media. Further, if any employees snapped photos or recorded video on their cell phones either during or after the incident, they should understand that the photos and video are considered evidence and should be turned over to the police rather than posted to their favorite social media sites. Even photos they may have snapped of employees standing around afterward will be wanted by the police who will view them to see if everyone in them can be identified as an associate and ensure that no shooter slipped out when employees were evacuated from the building.

SUPERVISOR AND MANAGEMENT TRAINING

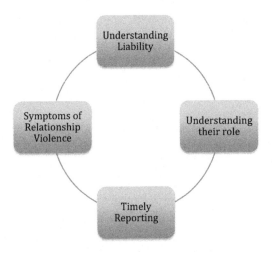

The Four Additional Components of Supervisor/Manager Training.

Managers and supervisors should receive the same training as nonsupervisory associates. In fact, if at all possible they should receive the training with the associates they supervise.

There are additional concepts that managers and supervisors need to understand and the first one is understanding liability. Whenever an incident occurs there are three questions that will be asked:

1. What did you know?
2. When did you know it?
3. What did you do about it?

If the answers are as follows, then there is probably liability that can result in regulatory fines as well lawsuits against the organization and possibly against individuals who knew about it, or should have known about it, and failed to take action to protect the people in the organization:

1. I knew something about it.
2. I knew something about it quite a while ago.
3. I did nothing about it.

Managers and supervisors also need to understand their roles once someone has come to them to report an issue.

- They should listen intently to show the associate that their concerns are being taken seriously. They should turn off their computers and forward their phones to voicemail so that there are no disturbances.
- They should be empathetic, but not sympathetic. They should thank the person for coming forward and appreciate the person's courage in doing so. They should indicate that they are very concerned about the allegations being made without passing judgment on them.
- They should explain what the process will be going forward, for example:
  - The complainant's information will be passed along to the human resource department, or whoever is the designee for such issues.
  - An investigation will be conducted to determine the facts.
  - The company will take appropriate action based on those facts.
  - The complainant will be notified when there is a resolution.
- After their meeting with the complainant, they should only divulge this information to those who have a need to know and not discuss it with subordinates, peers, their spouses, and so forth.
- The information needs to be forwarded to the appropriate people as soon as possible and preferably in person because these are usually sensitive issues and voicemail message and emails are not secure sources of communication. An in-person discussion also confirms that the person

to whom you are reporting the concerns understands the full weight of the situation. Confirmation that he or she understands the gravity of the issues cannot be obtained via an email or a phone message that is not read or heard right away.

- Timely reporting and the expedient initiation of the investigation is crucial for several reasons. Whatever is being reported, such as disruptive behavior, threats, or stalking, usually has to get really bad before it is reported. In our experience once the situation has been reported, you can expect that it has been going on for at least six months before anyone decided to lodge a formal complaint and, now that the complaint has been lodged, the complainant is waiting to see what the organization does about it. Also, any lapse in time before the investigation is initiated is time that the problem can escalate. Remember, once the organization is notified of a potential problem, the clock is ticking on the three questions that determine liability: What did you know, when did you know it, and what did you do about it?

Finally, as relationship abuse and violence is the most common issue that the company will face, the managers should be well aware of their symptoms as outlined in Chapter 5:

1. **Fatigue, tardiness, or unexplained absences:** The abuse, be it verbal or physical, frequently occurs at night and is often alcohol infused. It may begin at midnight or one o'clock in the morning and last for an hour or longer. Once the abuser falls asleep, the victim is racked with fear and adrenaline and cannot easily fall asleep. Once the alarm clock goes off, the victim may have had less than two hours sleep and this will manifest itself in either being very groggy at work, late, or absent from work altogether.

2. **Withdrawal from interactions with other employees:** The victim of relationship abuse is frequently very near a breakdown, and a simple question from a coworker such as, "How are you doing?" can be all it takes for the victim to collapse in tears. To defend themselves from breakdown, victims erect emotional walls and create emotional distance from their work associates.

3. **Low self-esteem:** The abuser inundates the victim with negative messages that the victim is worthless, stupid, unable to make decisions, unable to handle his or her own finances, and couldn't survive without the abuser. These messages coupled with the victim's perceived inability to escape from the relationship can be a severe detriment to the victim's self-esteem.

4. **Not taking a lunch break:** There can be several reasons for not taking a lunch break. The victim may lack an appetite because of the abuse or fatigue. The victim may not take a lunch break because he or she doesn't want to be around other employees as noted in first symptom. The victim may not take a lunch break as the abuser is controlling the finances and is not giving the victim funds to buy a lunch or prepare a lunch at home.

5. **Receiving frequent cell phone calls that cause the victim to leave the work area:** There are usually two reasons for leaving the work area to take a call. The victim doesn't want coworkers to overhear the abuser yelling at him or her and/or the victim doesn't want coworkers to see him or her crying.

6. **Visible bruises or attempting to conceal bruises.** Concealment techniques may include the use of too much makeup, wearing jackets or other out-of-place garments to cover the bruises, or wearing sunglasses to conceal a black eye.

We would like to reiterate that your managers and supervisors should be observant of these symptoms as clusters of sustained changes to the person's normal behavior. There are many reasons why someone might be skipping lunches or have a visible bruise that don't involve domestic abuse.

ENDNOTES

[1] Pete J. Blair, *United States Active Shooter Events from 2000 to 2010: Training and Equipment Implications* (Texas State University, Advanced Law Enforcement Rapid Response Training, March 2012)

[2] "20 Years Later: Long Island Rail Road Shooting Remembered as the Day Killer Colin Ferguson Went Off the Rails," Associated Press, Friday, December 6, 2013 http://www.nydailynews.com/new-york/lirr-bloodbath-remembered-20-years-article-1.1539603

[3] Eric Schmitt, "Gunman Shoots at White House from Sidewalk," *New York Times Archives*, October 30, 1994 http://www.nytimes.com/1994/10/30/us/gunman-shoots-at-white-house-from-sidewalk.html

[4] "Tucson Gunman before Rampage: 'I'll see you on national TV,' Associated Press, April 11, 2014 http://www.cbsnews.com/news/jared-loughner-who-shot-gabrielle-giffords-in-tucson-ranted-online/

[5] Joe Kemp, "Surveillance Video Shows Armed Robber Tackled by Passengers aboard Seattle Bus," *New York Daily News*, Thursday, December 19, 2013 http://www.nydailynews.com/news/national/video-shows-armed-robber-tackled-passengers-seattle-bus-article-1.1552819

CHAPTER 10

The Situational Assessment and Management Team

"Any committee is only as good as the most knowledgeable, determined and vigorous person on it. There must be somebody who provides the flame."
—*Lady Bird Johnson*

"If you want to kill any idea in the world, get a committee working on it."
—*Charles Kettering*

Contents

Abstract

After training employees on the violence prevention program and giving particular attention to warning behaviors commonly associated with those moving toward violence, it is vital to build the team that will assess and manage the cases that are reported. We refer to these teams as the situational assessment and management (SAM) team. Such teams rightly would include responsible representatives from the various groups within the organization with the ability to make timely decisions, such as legal, security, human resources, and facilities. Each team member must be trained in the proper method of assessing and managing cases of disturbing or threatening behavior, and the team must work as one unit with input from all. The objectives of the team are twofold: (1) to prevent violence and (2) to respond both during and after an incident has occurred. These two components are also called *backstage* and *onstage*.

Keywords: intimidation; investigation of threats; investigation; situational assessment and management; threat assessment; threat management; threat response; violence prevention.

This chapter begins with two rather contradictory quotes, both of which have merit. Lady Bird Johnson is correct when she stated, "There must be somebody who provides the flame." If you are reading this book, then more than likely, you are the flame. But Charles Kettering's quote is also apropos. In many organizations, committees are where ideas go to die. The situational assessment and management (SAM) team, however, may be dealing with life and death issues, imminent threats, people who are in danger, and people who are in fear. A sluggish committee has no place in these situations. So how do you avoid the committee conundrum?

First, create a team, not a committee. Teams work together to accomplish specific goals and everyone on the team needs to understand that this team may be literally dealing with someone's life or death. Second, set ground rules for how the team will operate and have everyone sign off. You and your team are free to set your own ground rules, but some of your ground rules might include the following:

- A statement of purpose, which clearly outlines that the SAM team is to provide safety and security to the organization, and occasionally this must be done under dire circumstances. When dire circumstances are present, this becomes the team's priority above everything else in which the individual team members may be involved.
- Everyone gets to have a chance to speak and offer his or her opinion.
- Every opinion or idea has some merit and should be discussed.
- No plan will be perfect, so choose the best plan rather than waiting for a perfect plan to appear. If we were living in a perfect world, this team would not be needed.
- Sometimes a plan that accomplishes the goal of prevention or security may be labeled *unfair*, based on past practices and precedents. Remind everyone that you are not working in a perfect universe. It is unfair that this problem you are trying to solve came up and it is unfair that you have to make decisions that are not fair, but that's the situation that you are facing.
- Be able to articulate why you chose a particular plan.
- Understand the weaknesses of the plan and have backup tactics ready should a weakness be exploited.
- If a team member responds that something in the plan won't work, then that member should also offer an alternative which will.
- This team will be tackling issues that the organization has not confronted in the past. Therefore, when discussing the merits of a plan, a rationalization such as, "We've never done it this way in the past," is a moot point as the organization has never faced the current circumstances in the past either.
- If the team gets off course, then someone needs to call for a course correction.

Important note: If someone on the team cannot agree to the ground rules, doesn't want to be on the team, doesn't believe in the team's mission, or just doesn't believe that the team is necessary, then get that person off the team and find another member. Someone whose heart is not with the team will be a detractor, distraction, and detriment to the team's success.

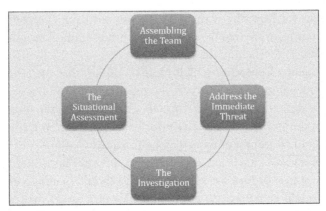

The Assessment Process

ASSEMBLING THE TEAM

The mission of your SAM team is twofold: (1) prevention and (2) response during and after a threat or violent incident.

The prevention or *backstage* mission is made up of four parts and will require representation from many functional groups. This may seem like too many people to have involved in your team; you might imagine that this many people might have a hard time finding agreement on all of the issues. There is some truth to this, however, without their direct participation, each of these functional groups is capable of throwing rationalizations, objections, and denials at your proposals later on. It is better to have them onboard at the beginning when they will have the benefit of participating in all of the discussions and agreements that are made by the SAM team. Also, they are participating in the backstage portion of the mission, and although there is some time sensitivity to their mission, they are not the portion of the team that is dealing with an imminent threat, which will be a part of a smaller and more focused group.

Backstage Team and Tasks

We recommend that the following backstage tasks should be carried out by the backstage team, who are members of different functional groups in the business.

Enhancing Policies, Procedures, and Processes

Human resources—In most organizations, the human resource team is the gatekeeper of policies and they are the most familiar with how policies are written, approved, and disseminated to the rest of the organization. Additionally, they must approve any policies that touch the associates of the organization.

Employee relations and legal—The employee relations and legal departments sometimes have the same function. Not all organizations have both departments, but representatives from either or both departments need to be a part of the team to ensure that all recommended policies, procedures, and processes are legal and do not violate any laws, government regulations, or collective bargaining agreements.

Risk—The risk department should be included as they usually have the most interaction with the Occupational Safety and Health Administration (OSHA). As they will be the first part of your organization approached by OSHA to audit or investigate your violence prevention plan, their input will be invaluable.

Security—Because the security department is in charge of the safekeeping of your staff and premises, their expertise in all facets of physical security and investigations is tantamount.

Operations—Many times the operations office is overlooked, but they are the ones who will feel the brunt of any changes. If the recommended policies, procedures, and processes are not operationally practical, they will not be executed effectively, thus voiding all of the work by the backstage team and rendering your violence prevention plan ineffective.

Enhancing Physical Security

Security—The security team is knowledgeable of the gaps in physical security and will have suggestions for contractors and hardware that will remedy the issues.

Employee relations and legal—Similar to their function regarding policies, procedures, and processes, the employee relations or legal department's participation is necessary to ensure that all recommended physical security enhancements are legal and do not violate any laws, government regulations, or collective bargaining agreements.

Facilities management—The most common physical security enhancements are made to video recording and access control systems. Sometimes the facility may be getting these systems for the first time; others may be getting a larger, state-of-the-art system. Regardless, any changes or additions to the premises necessitate that facilities management be a part of the discussion to ensure that the premises can accommodate the systems that are being proposed.

Information technology—Any hardware or software enhancements will involve information technology (IT), whether it is the networking of video and alarm systems or server connectivity for a new access control systems. The IT team needs to be in on the beginning of any systems-related discussions.

Construction—If anything is going to be physically installed, such as a conduit run, or if any alterations are made to the facility, the construction team needs to be included in the early discussions in order to make your installations go as smoothly as possible.

Finance—As with everything you try to do in an organization, it always comes down to money. If you are lucky enough to have been granted a budget, there will frequently be overruns. If you haven't been given a budget, you will need to find money somewhere. This is where a savvy finance representative is extremely beneficial. This individual may be able to find budgeted funds somewhere that are not being used or are being underused. A good finance person can save the day!

Enhancing Staff and Management Training

Human resources and staff member education—Larger organizations generally have an education department solely committed to the development of training programs for their associates. In smaller companies, the development of training programs may fall within the human resource department. In either regard, you need to have the gatekeeper of the organization's training function on board.

Security—The members of the security department will have much of the content expertise for the training program and thus belong on the portion of the team that is developing the training.

Operations—Operations needs to be a part of the training development team to ensure that the way the training will be delivered is feasible to work within the constraints of the operations of the business. This is not to say that they can or should veto the training, but if the training format or length of the training cannot practically be executed within the business, then the members of the operations department need to articulate those reasons and help find a solution to those problems.

Finance—As with physical security, finance is necessary to help you find any funding that you may need for the training program.

Onstage Team and Tasks

We recommend that the part of your SAM team that will be responding to threats and has what we refer to as the *onstage* mission responsibilities, be made up of representatives from four groups: security, human resources, legal department, and operations.

1. *Security*—The security team will be responsible for investigating the threat and the person making the threat. They will also play a role in helping to determine how best to respond and manage the threat.
2. *Human resources and/or employee benefits*—The human resource and/or employee benefits team will help put together the threat response and management plan. They will also be key in helping to some fundamental components, such as severance packages and psychological counseling plans.
3. *Employee relations and/or legal*—The employee relations and/or legal department representatives will also play a key role in the development of response and management plans from their perspective of ensuring that everything being done does not violate any laws, government regulations, or collective bargaining agreements.
4. *Operations*—Operations needs to be a part of the response and management plans as operations will usually play a part in the plan's execution or be affected by the plan. The team members from operations need to understand what is being proposed, understand how it will affect operations, and make sure the plan is executable by their staff. If the plan is not operationally feasible, you need to know that as the plan is being formulated so you can find options to work around the issues. You don't want to spend valuable time putting together a plan only to find out at the point of execution that is not feasible.

ADDRESSING THE IMMEDIATE THREAT

This is a fairly short discussion. If the threat is imminent, what needs to be done to immediately secure the premises? For example,

- Do you need armed security?
- Are off-duty police officers needed?
- Should the facility be put on lockdown?

One of the most overlooked tactics is to remove the person being targeted from the facility. In instances of pursuit by a former relationship partner or coworker, the quickest way to make the facility safe is to remove the intended subject. The former relationship partners and coworkers have an uncanny ability to know when their target is in the building and when they are not—so get them out, send them home, send them on vacation, send them on an extended business trip, and so forth This is one of those instances where your response plan might be considered to be *unfair* to the targeted associate. It might be, however, it is also unfair that this individual's presence on the premises puts everyone else's lives at risk. As mentioned earlier, there are no perfect plans so choose the best plan available.

THE INVESTIGATION

A prompt and thorough investigation is necessary to limit the liability exposure that your organization may eventually face. It shows that you handled the complaint in a timely manner; it proves that prompt remedial action was taken; it proves that the company's internal complaint procedure is effective; and it shows that appropriate decisions were made via the facts determined by your thorough investigation.

The first rule of investigations, situational assessments, and building a threat response plan is a simple one: Make sure that what you do does not make the situation worse. Let's start with some bad news: You can't learn the art and science of conducting investigations, interviewing people, and detecting deception from a book. Whoever is conducting the investigation needs to be professionally trained, whether that individual is someone from your organization or a contracted third-party investigator. When we say professionally trained, we mean professionally trained in the art and science of interviewing and interrogation and professionally trained to conduct investigations and interviews in the private sector. Agents of the government, such as law enforcement and military investigators, have an expanded range of authority and power to investigate criminal or national security matters that are not granted to private sector investigators. For example, if the person making the threat does not work for your organization, you as an agent of a private sector business, do not have the power or authority to make that person submit to your interview. Whoever is conducting your investigation needs to understand and abide by the differences between public sector and private sector power of authority. There are also people who have not been properly trained who tend to use investigation techniques garnered from movies and television shows, which are at best unethical and in the worst case, illegal. Those techniques include, but are not limited to:

- Promises of leniency that the investigator never intends to keep
- Intimidation by threat of extreme prosecution or harsh treatment
- Inferences to vast amounts of nonexisting, incriminating evidence

If detrimental employment action resulted from confessions or other information gained via these tactics, the business can be exposed to legal liability and damage to its reputation and brand. The courts will most certainly rule that the investigator used tactics that could cause an innocent person to confess in order to avoid the realization of the threats that had been made. They can also take a person who already perceives that he or she has a serious grievance with the organization and escalate this individual's behavior to the point of violent actions up to and including homicide. If an associate, who already exhibits the warning behaviors discussed in Chapters 5 and 6, perceives that his or her career is being harmed by a supervisor or coworker and now experiences this type of intimidation at the hands of someone representing the upper management of the company, then that individual may feel that the only alternative left is some type of violence. Having lost any hope of getting a fair shake from the company can leave these individuals in very dangerous states of mind.

Business-related investigations must be handled with tact, they must be handled ethically, and they must allow the person being investigated to present his or her side of the story. There are a number of companies that teach the skills and ethical tactics required for a private sector investigation. One of the standouts is Wicklander-Zulawski & Associates (www.w-z.com). They offer their seminars all across the United States. If you want to get training for your organization, you can access their schedule via their website to see when they will be holding a seminar near you. Additionally, if you have a number of people within your organization you desire to train, arrangements can be made for them to come to you.

While we are not going to attempt to teach interviewing and investigation techniques via this chapter, we do wish to discuss some things that should be included in investigations of threats and those that pose them. One of the very first things that should be done is to trace the threat back to its point of origination. You should understand that by the time the threat is related to you, it is at least fourth-hand information and everyone who passed it along has added to or subtracted from the original statement that has been considered to be a threat. (See the following box for an example.) Some people are predisposed to panicking when a supposed threat is made, so the threat may get embellished as it passes through their hands. Other people may be in denial that an act of violence could ever happen where they work, so they may downplay the threats when they pass them along.

A client called us on a Wednesday afternoon regarding a threat on a vice president's life made by an employee who had been suspended and knew, based on his past infractions, that he was going to be fired. The alleged threat was made on the prior Friday afternoon shortly after the employee was suspended. The employee was to come in this Friday, one-and-a-half days away, where his employment disposition would be rendered.

Since Monday the company had been talking to the police department about the threat and, at the point where we were brought in, the police department was trying to determine the best places to have their SWAT team deployed in and around the building.

As our first course of action, we traced the threat back to the point of origin and found that it was seventh-hand information by the time it reached the vice president. Further, we found that the suspended employee had made no direct threat. A coworker of the suspended employee was talking to the supervisor about organizational and operational changes that were primarily being seen as negative by many of the associates. The coworker stated that someone like the suspended associate could come in and shoot the place up. The suspended employee never made a threat; the statement was embellished as it was passed up the line; and a lot of people wasted a lot of time and suffered a great deal of anxiety over nothing. (And yes, we did investigate, interview, and assess the coworker to see if he posed a danger and he did not. He was confused and anxious about the business changes and needed some time with the human resource department to explain what was going on and answer his questions.)

The moral of the story is "Always trace the threat back to the point of origin."

Background Checks

The next piece we want to discuss is conducting background checks. At some point during the investigation or situational assessment phase, someone will ask about conducting a background check on the subject being investigated and assessed. A background check should be done, but you need to understand the limitations of the background check. The first thing to understand is that past history is not as relevant as recent history. For example, the United States fought two wars against England—in 1776 and in 1812. *That is past history.* In recent history Great Britain is our closest ally. So if you are conducting a background check on a 40-year-old man who has a conviction for assault and battery that occurred when he was 18 and drunk at a party, his history actually shows that he has *not* chosen violence as a means of problem resolution for the past 22 years. The only important part to note about past history is what, if anything, the subject says about it.

If the individual talks about it, does the person accept responsibility for his or her actions or does the person blame his or her past problems on other people or institutions, such as the police or a prior employer?

Conversely, recent history is very important. For example, we were called to consult on an organization's associate who threatened to kill his manager. In looking at the associate's address, it was recognized as being a halfway house for parolees just out of prison. A background check showed that the associate had been paroled 2 months earlier after serving 18 months for throwing his former manager through a plate glass window. That recent history was very useful in determining whether this individual was capable of violence and it was also useful in getting his parole violated and having him sent back to prison.

The next thing to understand about background checks is that a lack of violent history does not mean that the person is not capable of violence. We can find examples of this all through history, but let's start our examination with the Columbine High School killers. Prior to their shootings at Columbine, did they have a recorded history of violence? What about the Virginia Tech killer or the Boston Marathon bombers or the Aurora, Colorado, movie theater killer, or the killer at Mother Emmanuel Church in Charleston, South Carolina? We could go on, but the point is clear. Just because someone hasn't been violent in the recent past doesn't mean the person can't become violent in the future. As we will discuss in the section on situational assessments, the most important factors to investigate are the person's current words and actions, the context in which those words and actions are being made, and the environment in which the person making the threats is immersed.

In the following sections, we'll discuss the elements that should be present in a thorough investigation.

Guiding Principles

We have determined that there are three principles to guide your investigation:

- Principle 1—Your purpose is to reveal the truth.
- Principle 2—Be objective and do not let yourself be influenced by the conjecture or bias of someone else. Do not go into the investigation with any preconceived notion of what the truth is and do not be influenced by anyone who makes statements of bias toward anyone whom you will be interviewing. In our experience, whenever someone tells us, "she is making this all up" or "he is bad news and we need to get rid of him," they are dead wrong in about 50% of the incidents. Let the facts bring you to your own valid conclusions.

- Principle 3—Conduct and document investigations that are thorough, fair, and will stand up under any scrutiny. If someone claims that unfair disciplinary actions were taken as a result of your investigation or, if a violent incident occurs and your organization is sued, your investigation will be put under a microscope. A clear and thoroughly documented report detailing your exhaustive investigation can stop claims of a negligent investigation dead in their tracks.

Reasons for a Prompt Investigation

There are several very important reasons why you should conduct an investigation as soon after an incident as possible:

- With each passing day, evidence begins to disappear either intentionally or by mistake. Documents get lost, electronic evidence gets deleted, or people discard the piece of evidence not realizing its importance.
- An early, thorough investigation leads to a better assessment of facts and liability so that your organization can make consistent and informed decisions
- A timely investigation helps protect you from accusations that you did not take the matter seriously.

Gathering Evidence

Depending on the nature of the investigation, there may be many different pieces of evidence to collect. Some, but by no means all, of the evidence available might include:

- The subject's personnel file that should contain his or her work history (including other places the person may have lived), performance appraisals, and any disciplinary history
- Incident reports detailing accurate accounts of any incidents that happened in the past
- Documented recollections of witnesses who can provide statements into current issues, including additional information about the demeanor of the subject as well as any outside interests or recent behavioral changes
- The schedule of who was working when incidents occurred and may be potential additional witnesses
- And electronic media, which may provide greater insight into mindset of the subject, such as:
    - Voicemails
    - Emails

- Text messages
- Social media screenshots

If a video record exists, it is a key evidentiary resource that must be retrieved and protected as soon as possible. The inability to provide the video of the incident may tend to create a perception that the organization is hiding something. It is always best to check video records of all areas, not just the one in question, so that you can:

- Determine if a video record of the alleged issue exists anywhere on the premises. Failure to do so means that your investigation was not thorough.
- Identify who was in the area where the incident occurred, as they should be interviewed as potential witnesses.
- Identify where other people were at the time of the incident as this might rule them out as witnesses.
- Confirm or refute any current or future statements of fact.

And again, the video records should be saved regardless of whether or not they prove the allegation being investigated. If, and this is very important, the incident was of a serious or sensitive nature, such as an incident resulting in the death or serious injury of someone, the system's hard drive should be swapped out and saved to preserve the integrity of the recorded evidence.

Interviewing the Alleged Victim

Before interviewing the alleged victim, it is important to recognize if the alleged victim is, in fact, being harassed or abused. This is a delicate subject that the alleged victim would probably prefer not talking about, especially to a stranger. The alleged victim is undoubtedly experiencing some anxiety about coming forward. Recognize this and thank the individual for having the strength to talk to you. Be empathetic but neutral until all of the facts are revealed.

Most victims are concerned about retaliation from the accused or even from the business in terms of their peers, supervisors, and managers. Reassure them that your organization has a policy of no retaliation (see Chapter 1; this is OSHA mandated), however, make sure they understand that you cannot protect them if they do not report any perceived acts of retaliation.

If the person being accused is or used to be an employee, you will want to determine if there is any prior history or relationship between the alleged victim and the accused. You will also want to determine if there is any ulterior motive for making a claim against the accused, such as a desire to transfer to another department or facility or to provide leverage against any poor performance reviews. Always ask if there is physical evidence, such as notes, cards, emails, text messages, social media posting, and so forth. In today's world of Internet communication, there may be an abundance of electronically stored evidence, so be thorough in your pursuit of any possible physical or electronic evidence that may be available.

Interviewing the Accused

As mentioned earlier in this chapter, if the person accused of threats or other misconduct is not an employee of your organization, you may not be able to interview this individual. If you cannot interview the person, your investigation will center on interviews with the alleged victim and witnesses, background information that can be obtained and assessed, and physical or electronic evidence relating to the threat(s) and disturbing behavior.

If you can interview the accused, then this is where your investigator must be well trained to understand the ethical tactics that can be used and experienced enough to know how to control the interview, detect deception, and motivate the subject to be truthful. Unfortunately as mentioned earlier, you cannot learn this in a book. Please get your investigation staff professionally trained.

Final Thoughts on Investigations

You may be called on to testify about the finding of your investigation and how you conducted your investigation. You will need to be able to articulate good reasons for the determinations that were taken as a result of your investigation and articulate good reasons for everything you did during the interview, such as why you interviewed some people and not others. Because of that, treat every interview as if it may be the last time you may be able to talk to the person. The individuals might move away or decide not to talk to you again. Before ending an interview, take a moment to think and determine if there is anything else about which you need to inquire.

Final things to remember include the following:

- Precise factual details are important; conjecture or opinions have very little value when they are not backed up by facts.
- Beware of the most common and serious omissions and mistakes that mark your investigation as *not* being thorough:
  - A comment or *fact* is mentioned in the case report but not documented in any statements. If the person who supplied that fact will not document it in writing, then that should be so noted in the

case report. Otherwise there is no documentary evidence to support what is being purported as factual evidence.

- Allegations mentioned verbally or in statements are not followed up on and/or the follow-up is not documented in the case report. Any allegations by anyone interviewed, whether the allegations are made in writing or made verbally, must be followed up on and so documented in your case report.
- Names mentioned during an interview as having been involved, as having witnessed, as having knowledge, or as having given permission or direction are not followed up on and/or not documented in the case report.

In other words before your investigation is completed, make sure to follow up on any and all loose ends!

CONDUCTING THREAT ASSESSMENTS

It is important to recognize that many threats are uttered by people who are not actually capable of committing an act of violence. The threats are spoken out of anger and frustration and are only meant to intimidate and/or cause anxiety. Proper assessment training is needed to be able to determine which threats are serious and which aren't. Unfortunately, this cannot be learned from a book. We cannot overstate the necessity of a professional threat assessment, and your relationship with a threat assessment professional should be established sooner rather than later. The moment a death threat is uttered is the wrong time to start vetting assessment companies and having your legal department begin combing through their contracts. We also recognize, however, that in some instances, the threat is imminent and you may not have the time to get a threat assessment team on site. So, while professional assessment training is needed for your staff and/or a professional assessment company should be on call, there are a few key components to a threat assessment that we can give you.

Here are seven important questions to be answered in the course of your threat assessment. You may not have the ability to get answers for all of them, but if you can answer three or four of them, you can generally get enough of a picture to determine your next steps.

1. *What are the current words being used in the threat and what are the threatener's current actions?* The stakes are high if the threatener is using profane language, making direct threats, and becoming violent with inanimate objects.

2. *What is the context in which the threats and actions are taking place?* Context is everything. Words or actions taken out of context can twist their meaning. If someone in the office remarks to another employee something such as, "I'm going to you on Saturday," then that sounds pretty bad. However if the threat was made in the context of a golf match they have arranged for Saturday morning, then no real homicidal intention is present.

3. *What is going on in the environment in which the threatener is living?* Are there additional stressors in the person's life? For example,

Is the person about to lose his or her job?

Has the individual lost a loved one? Has the person been jilted by a lover or spouse?

Has the individual recently found him- or herself in dire financial straits and is about to lose his or her home or have his or her car repossessed?

Have there been recent acts of workplace violence reported in the media?

4. *Does the threatener have a perceived grievance against the company or someone connected to the company and feels that he or she "owes them a bloodbath"?*

5. *Does the threatener feel that there are no other resources available to him or her other than violence?* Has the individual tried to resolve this issue through the company or other avenues and been rejected?

6. *Does the threatener have any fear of the penalties for his or her actions?* Check witnesses and social media pages to see if the person expressed feelings of martyrdom or expressed no fear of the police, courts, and prison time.

7. *Does the threatener have the capacity to make the threat a reality?* Has the individual recently acquired the implements to carry out the threats or does the person have any special training that would help him or her accomplish the threat? For example, if a threat to blow up the threatener's manager's car is made, does the threatener have the training and access to explosives to actually make that threat a reality? Do not ignore that threat until you have answered those questions.

Let's apply these seven questions to the case study presented in Chapter 1 and see how it could have been assessed. The following box is a recap of what was commonly known at the time of Amanda Brown's murder.

Amanda Brown was divorced. Her ex-husband had a long history of assaulting her both at her apartment and her place of work. In fact she had been transferred from one work location to another facility because he physically assaulted her at her prior work location so often. Unfortunately, he soon found out her new work location and the assaults continued, although not so frequently as it was further away from where he lived.

Amanda just moved to a new apartment further away from him and a judge had just granted her request to have her temporary restraining order made permanent. As soon as her ex-husband was served with the restraining order, he began calling her place of employment and demanding to speak with her. Although she was not at work that day, she but did stop by to give a human resource representative her new address and a copy of the permanent restraining order because the workplace was named in the court document. On the following day Amanda's ex-husband called her workplace, asking for her and she declined to speak to him. So, now knowing that she was there, her ex-husband came down to the workplace and stabbed her to death.

Let's see how many of the seven questions can be answered in order to determine an appropriate course of action.

1. What are the current words being used in the threat and what are her ex-husband's current actions? *Actually it is not known if a threat has been made, but it is known that he is calling incessantly and sounds enraged to the receptionist who takes his calls.*

2. What is the context in which the threats and actions are taking place? *It is known or should have been known that Amanda just moved and got a permanent restraining order, therefore the only place her ex-husband knows to find her is at the workplace.*

3. What is going on in the environment in which her ex-husband is living? *Amanda had divorced him and has now gotten a permanent restraining order barring him from making any contact with her.*

4. Does her ex-husband have a perceived grievance against the company or someone connected to the company and feels that he "owes them a bloodbath"? *He has no grievance against the company, but his past history shows that he physically assaulted Amanda on many occasions.*

5. Does Amanda's ex-husband feel that there are no other resources available to him other than violence? *A civil court took her side and granted her divorce and a criminal court took her side and issued her a restraining order that was delivered by a sheriff's deputy. In his mind, the entire justice system is against him.*

6. Does her ex-husband have any fear of the penalties for his actions? *This is tough to completely know, although he assaulted her during the tenure of the temporary restraining order.*

7. Does Amanda's ex-husband have the capacity to make the threat a reality? *Well, we do not know of any direct threat, but we do know that he is calling incessantly and is enraged.*

Based on what you have garnered from answering the preceding seven questions, which of the following would you do?

1. Not think much of it because the facility is in a low-crime neighborhood and, after all, Amanda had the permanent restraining order to protect her.
2. Notify the police and ask them to frequently drive by the facility.
3. Tell Amanda to stay home until you have more time to assess the situation, assess her ex-husband, and determine an appropriate course of action.

If you answered "C" then congratulations, you just saved Amanda Brown's life.

CHAPTER 11

High-Risk Terminations and Building an Enhanced Security Plan

"As a goalkeeper you need to be good at organizing the people in front of you and motivating them. You need to see what's going on and react to the threats. Just like a good manager in business."

—*Peter Shilton*

"I felt a great disturbance in the Force…"

—*Obi-Wan Kenobi*

Contents

Abstract

A properly designed and executed violence prevention program can be highly effective in reducing the occurrence of violence but cannot guarantee that employees at risk for violence will not need to be expelled from the organization for a variety of causes, including poor performance or inappropriate or threatening behavior. In fact, a strong program will shed light on such behavior and can result in such terminations. Many organizations do not handle these meetings or deliver the termination message in a way that mitigates the risk of immediate or future violence. Following sound advice at this critical time can help minimize this threat and ensure the separated employee who is posing a threat leaves for good. This goes hand in hand with the need for the creation of an enhanced security plan during and after the high-risk termination.

Keywords: anger management counseling; disturbing behavior; employee counseling; enhanced security plan; firing manager; high-risk termination; psychological counseling; risk of violence; severance package; termination meeting; warning signs of violence.

The preceding quote from Peter Shilton is pretty close to the desired goal in managing threats and disturbing behavior. It would be spot on if he said, "You need to see what's going on and react to disturbing behavior before it escalates into a threat." Your goal should be to sense the disturbances in your organization's environment just as Obi-Wan could feel the great disturbance in the Force. But unfortunately you can't do this on your own. Everybody in your organization has to be onboard in order to detect disturbing behavior in its early stages and be in position to intervene before the behavior turns violent. This is why you train people on the warning signs, make them responsible to report them, and provide them with a safe and easy vehicle by which they can express their concerns. The earlier you can detect a problem, the safer and easier it will be remedy the issue(s).

Everything in preceding Chapters 4 through 10 has been focused on helping you develop an effective plan to prevent, intervene, and mitigate threats and violence. It's time to begin to discuss the steps that will need to be taken if the methods to correct the threatener's behavior have not been productive. The best place to start is with handling high-risk terminations, however, as you go through the rest of this chapter, it is important to remember that this information is only to be used in terminations where your assessment shows there is a potential for violence. These steps would be highly excessive if used with someone who has chronic punctuality problems but poses no threat to anyone in the business.

The first thing to be done is to select the best person in the organization to handle the termination meeting. In most organizations, the subject's manager or someone from the human resource department usually handles terminations. Although this works for routine separations, high-risk terminations require that the person handling the meeting have certain qualities. The person handling high-risk terminations should be someone with the following abilities.

- The person should have the experience and maturity to maintain the confidentiality regarding the termination he or she will be handling.
- The person should be respected by the person being terminated. Do not use someone who has an axe to grind. If the person chosen to conduct the termination says something akin to "Boy! I've been waiting for this day. This guy has been a pain in the neck for a long time and firing him will make my day," then this is the wrong choice. This person will most likely express these sentiments verbally or nonverbally during the separation meeting, potentially escalating the risk of the firing.
- The person should be at the appropriate managerial level to conduct terminations. If the person handling the termination is not someone who normally conducts them, then the subject will realize that his or her intimidations have struck a nerve within the company and realize that people are afraid of him or her. This will only motivate the subject to continue his or her pattern of harassment and intimidation.
- Not surprisingly, the person should be able to handle intimidation and maintain his or her composure. Just as in the preceding point, if the subject realizes that people are afraid of him or her, then you can expect the subject's behavior to continue and/or escalate during the termination meeting. This is where experience and maturity becomes a necessary asset. The firing manager must keep the meeting on track and not become distracted by the subject's attempts to convince him or her that the termination is unwarranted and unjust. The firing manager has to be tactful, but clear. In other words, the subject must understand that he or she has been terminated. We have been consulted on situations where the subject's termination was worded so vaguely the person did not realize he or she had been terminated.

If it is difficult to find one person who has all of these abilities. Assess which of these qualities will be of most importance in handling the termination at hand and that will help advance your search. Along with selecting the best person to handle the termination, there are additional considerations.

It is best to handle the termination at the end of the subject's shift, preferably on the day before the subject's next scheduled day off. Make sure that anyone the subject may blame for his or her problems have left the premises. The reason for handling the termination at the end of the shift is so that the terminated employee will be going home at the regular time as usual. That way the person has the ability to maintain the routine he or she would normally follow. This is the same reason to conduct the termination at the end of shift prior to the subject's day off.

There is another school of thought that prefers to terminate at the beginning of the shift as soon as the decision to terminate is made. This is done so that the person who was fired can go right down to the unemployment office to apply for benefits. It is rare, however, that the first thing someone who has been fired will apply for unemployment benefits. Also it is rare, in today's day and age that someone has to actually go to the employment office to apply for benefits. The application for benefits can usually be accomplished online.

The determining factor of whether to terminate as soon as the decision has been made or wait until the day before the individual's next day off should be made during your situational assessment. If your assessment indicates that the person is an imminent threat, then conduct the termination immediately and execute your enhanced security plan.

As mentioned earlier you don't want the subject running into anyone that he or she may blame for his or her termination when leaving the premises. If the individual blames many of his or her coworkers or your assessment shows that violence may be imminent, then another course of action is to handle the termination offsite. This could be another company facility where the individual doesn't know anyone or you could rent a small conference room at a hotel. Whenever we mention the latter part of that statement during live training sessions, there are those who are concerned that the subject would get violent in the public area of the hotel. In our experience, this has not occurred, nor have we seen any such reports in the media. We feel this is because the subject of the termination has no grievance with anyone in the hotel.

The next consideration is to determine what will be said during the termination meeting. It is best to have a script that the manager will follow in order to keep the discussion on track. There is usually no need to cite specific points as to why the subject is being terminated, as the termination should not be a complete surprise. Unless the organization has been negligent in reviewing performance and documenting problematic behavior, the subject is well acquainted with the issues that have led to the termination meeting. The individual may not agree with the issues, but the subject should be very familiar with them. Additionally, if you list specific violations of policy, you can expect to become engaged in an argument regarding the validity of the individual charges. The subject will attempt to convince you to continue his or her employment and/or demonstrate how coworkers, supervisors, and managers have conspired against him or her.

At this point you have selected a termination manager who the subject respects, which will inhibit violence. You are handling the termination in as neutral a location as possible (not a location that will cause the subject anxiety, such as having to face coworkers or come in contact with someone who the individual blames for his or her termination), and you are not going to cite specific violations that have caused the termination. Now we need to discuss how the termination manager should begin the meeting. The following are recommended phrases that can be worked into the script for the manager to follow:

- "Clearly things have not turned out as either you or the company expected when you were hired."
- "I know you are not happy here, and in instances such as this, frequently, the best thing we can do is allow you to start over fresh and find another place of employment where your skills and experience can flourish."
- "We're here today to discuss a decision that the company has made and explain how we can help you move forward (more on this in the "Softening the Landing" section).

Important note: If, during the termination meeting, the subject wants go to the bathroom reply, "you know, I need to go too" and escort the subject there. If the subject wants to go to his or her locker or desk or go get something out of his or her vehicle, do not let the person do that. If the subject demands to leave the meeting, you certainly cannot force the person to stay, but you can decline to allow the individual to go back into the office facility and require that the person leaves. Once the person has left the building you should immediately lockdown the perimeter of the facility. Discretely monitor the person's outside movements from inside the facility and execute your enhanced security plan.

SOFTENING THE LANDING

We have frequently seen that the way the termination is handled can inhibit both imminent, as well as possible, future violence. If it is handled appropriately, the subject may just realize that this job has not been the right fit and will realize that moving on would be in his or her best interest. Not to mislead you, this works best if you discover the problem with this associate early on and separate this person before his or her behavior escalates and feelings of persecution mature.

Handle the person with dignity. Being fired is humiliating even if the person deserves to be fired, and most people will not feel that they deserve it. Have you ever heard of someone who was fired who stood up and declared, "Boy, I got exactly what I deserved!" Another consideration along these lines is determining who else will be in the room when the termination is conducted. Our advice to clients is that no more than two people be in the room. This will usually consist of the manager conducting the firing and someone from human resources to explain any termination benefits and answer any questions the subject may have about final pay, vacation accrual, and so forth. We advise against having security personnel or police officers in the room. This only tends to further strip the terminated associate of dignity and may tend to escalate future behavior toward the company. This doesn't mean that security or police officers cannot be nearby. Additionally, if your assessment shows that violence is very probable at the termination meeting, then police officers in clothing that blends in with the company dress code can be included in the meeting under the pretext that the officer is an assistant to the human resource representative.

Also termination benefits can go a long way in helping to soften the landing. Because you've told the individual that this job is not a good fit and you express the hope that this individual finds a new job, then you should consider offering to pay for job placement counseling. Getting the person into psychological counseling is also very effective in dampening outrage. You cannot order the person into anger management counseling, but you can find a softer way of making the statement, such as, "We all know that you have differences with some of the other staff members and we would like to have you see some people who can help you find alternative ways to handle differences when they come up. We all want you to be successful in the future, so we are offering to pay for six months of visits with these counselors."

Another consideration is to offer the person a severance package. You may have the subject tell you that money does not matter and that he or she is only out for justice but, in the end, it usually just comes down to money, and the offer of a severance package is frequently a very effective tactic. There will be those within your organization who find this suggestion to be aberrant and say that paying someone who is harassing the organization to leave it sends the wrong message. In the past, we were fortunate to work with a general counsel who said, "I would rather write a check for $100,000 every time than risk a murder" or, as he stated to someone who balked about giving a disgruntled and potentially violent employee a severance package, "I am not going to risk a homicide just so you can prove a point." We think it is important to note that we have never had to write a check for $100,000; usually these matters can be settled for around 10% of that figure. We have also had executives within an organization rationalize against a severance package by remarking, "So you're saying that any time an employee is not happy with the company, we'll hand out a severance package?" Our response is always the same, "Yes, if our assessment of the person shows evidence that there is a real potential for violence." The severance package offers the subject and the company a couple of benefits. It allows the terminated associate time to locate a job without worrying about his or her immediate financial obligations; in other words, it is a stress reliever. And if a job is found that requires relocation, the severance payment can help make that relocation possible. You *want* the terminated employee to move away so it behooves you to *help* the subject make it possible.

AFTER THE TERMINATION IS OVER

Once the termination is over, your job is not done. You must debrief the person(s) who conducted the termination and perform an assessment of the subject's behavior. What was his or her demeanor? Did the subject issue any indirect or direct threats toward the company or any coworkers, supervisors, or managers? What was the exact language he or she used? Did the subject make any mention about what he or she would do next or relate any thoughts about future plans? Do not worry if the subject mentioned bringing a lawsuit. Many more people threaten than actually follow through, and filing a lawsuit is an acceptable, nonviolent response to termination. However, if the terminated employee does file a lawsuit, you should be monitoring this person during the proceedings and assessing his or her behavior so that you can make informed decisions about the facility's security.

Another component of your posttermination plan is assigned and scheduled communication with the intended victims and the facility in which they work. Has the terminated associate called anyone? Has the terminated associate shown up? Is anyone experiencing harassing phone calls at work or at home? Has anyone experienced any property damage? As mentioned in the first sentence, you must assign and schedule someone to conduct the ongoing follow-up communication because, even if you have instructed intended victims to call you if there are any issues, the intended victims and the managers of their facility will invariably not contact you. They mean to but they get busy and forget or they think they will be bothering you. The only way you will be updated about any issues or problems will be if you initiate the communication.

During the posttermination phase, you may also find that you need to respond to the fears of your associates. We advise clients that their response should be handled with these four components:

1. *Empathy.* Listen and show your associates that you sincerely care about their well-being.
2. *Honesty.* Be honest about what you can do and what you cannot do for them.
3. *Actions.* Whatever you said that you could do, do it, do it right, and do it as fast as possible.
4. *Counseling.* Refer them to counseling through your employee assistance plan.

THE ENHANCED SECURITY PLAN

At several points throughout this book we have referred to an *enhanced security plan*. We have mentioned some of the components in previous chapters but to concisely define the enhanced security plan we will divide it into three components:

1. *Tight physical security.* One of the first tasks mentioned in this book was to assess your physical security and determine where your gaps lay. Primarily, you should have identified lapses in closed-circuit television coverage and lapses in access control. If you have already bridged these gaps, then you should audit them to ensure that the actual level of security is as tight as you assume it to be.
2. *Armed and appropriately trained security presence.* This is important and it is an area where organizations tend to scrimp because it can be expensive. However, if you have assessed that violence is probable and perhaps imminent, then you have to determine whether your current proprietary or contracted security personnel will be adequate. If they are unarmed, then they will not be. If they are armed but have not had the tactical training necessary to protect your facility, then they will still not be

adequate. We advise clients to hire off-duty police officers or contract with security companies that have off-duty police officers or former military specialists on staff.

3. *A plan to monitor the subject.* In every war since the beginning of recorded history, intelligence has assisted the military in thwarting enemy attacks. You need an intelligence plan as well. It should include inquiring as to whether or not the former associate is contacting anyone and setting up an email screen to make sure you see any incoming emails from the subject, and it should include monitoring the subject's online presence to see what he or she is talking about, his or her actions (Is the subject currently at Disneyland or do the photos show recent firearms acquisitions?), and whether or not the subject has put a manifesto online.

Hopefully, we have convinced you that you are not powerless and there are tools and tactics available to protect your organization.

CHAPTER 12

Managing the Aftermath of Violence

"The best laid plans of mice and men often go awry."
—Adapted from "To a Mouse" by Robert Burns

Contents

Abstract

Even the most robust and comprehensive workplace violence prevention and response programs cannot ensure that no acts of serious violence will ever occur on your premises. It is for this reason that such a program must include a detailed thoughtful plan for managing the situation after violence. There are many considerations but paramount must be a strong desire and plan to take care of those affected by the violence whether they are employees, visitors, customers, or those not affiliated with your organization in any way. Acting with confidence and certainty at such critical times defines an organization and leaves a lasting impression on all. While the implementation of such planning forces the organization to consider and plan for the unthinkable, failure to do so will undoubtedly mean a flawed, fractured response, which will not be forgotten or go unnoticed by a critical media.

Keywords: aftermath; anger; business recovery; denial; emotional turmoil; grief; homicide; investigation; law enforcement; public communication; public information officer; shock; shooting; training; trauma; violence; witness interviews.

There may be a time when, despite your planning and vigilance, violence still comes to visit. A common weak link is that you must rely on other people (and sometimes a vast number of people) to alert you to a threat or other disturbing circumstances and unfortunately, human beings are not perfect. There may also be a situation where an external threat exists of which no one in your organization is cognizant. Similar to the shooting of Transportation Security Administration (TSA) personnel at the Los Angeles International Airport detailed in Chapter 7, no one within TSA, the airport police, the Los Angeles Police Department, or anyone else working at the airport had any idea who the shooter was or that he had a grievance against the government. Friends and family members knew but, having no training, did not know what to do with the information in a timely manner that would have prevented the shootings and the one homicide.

So the remaining part of your planning efforts should focus on managing the aftermath of violence. As mentioned so many times earlier, after the event has occurred is the wrong time to develop your plan. Based on the circumstances of your incident, your plan can certainly be amended as necessary but you need to have a basic framework of what needs to be done. The tasks within the framework should be preassigned to individuals or functional groups so that they may begin executing responsibilities as soon as possible.

The five components of your aftermath recovery are shown in below figure. These components should be executed simultaneously, not

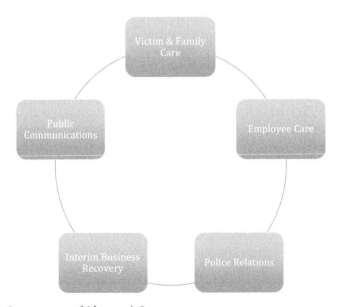

The Five Components of Aftermath Recovery

sequentially. We realize that it may not be possible or, depending on the circumstances, appropriate to do everything we discuss in the following sections. You will need to determine which of these makes sense for the situation to which you are responding.

VICTIM AND FAMILY CARE

The families of the victims will be going through many emotional phases, such as shock, denial, grief, and anger. They will be in an initial state of confusion and the family members may forget to take care of themselves. Additionally family members from outside of the area may be coming into town. So the first need they will have is lodging and food. If you have a corporate travel department or travel agent that you deal with, then this office or agent can be helpful in finding quality and economical lodging. Your travel department may even be able to negotiate a discount based on the circumstances and number of rooms needed. It would also be great if your organization could pick up a week or two of lodging for the immediate family. It is important to note that if you decided to pay for any of the lodging, you need to clearly set out the limitations on who you will be paying for (e.g. immediately family being mother, father, sister, and brother) and how long you will be picking up the tab.

Food will be the next thing with which you can be helpful. You can provide groceries for the in-town family and gift cards to local restaurants and fast food locations to those from out of town. Think of what the in-town families will need for the next two weeks, stock their pantries and don't forget beverages. The stress that they will be under can promote dehydration so make sure plenty of bottled water is included. Also provide an occasional catered meal that would accommodate the in-town and out-of-town family members. Be a gracious host. Similarly, provide the catering for any memorial or funeral services.

The family's emotional well-being should also be a priority. If the city or county does not provide victim counseling, then make counseling, via your employee assistance program provider, available to them and pick up the cost. They are going through a tremendous amount of stress, grief, and general emotional turmoil, so having the family meet with counselors through your program will be a huge benefit for them.

Money will be a large issue for them as well. You have picked up the tabs for meals, lodging, and counseling, but your employees may wish to help as well. Place donation jars at a few appropriate places around your facility and encourage your associates to donate the cost of a premium cup of coffee or the change from their lunch purchase.

If the victim has children, consider setting up a trust fund for them with a local bank; make a sizeable donation and publicize how the community can add to the fund. You might also consider other needs for the children, such as back-to-school clothing, school supplies, or holiday gifts if the incident took place prior to these events.

Have you ever called a health care insurance agency regarding a claim and the only result was personal frustration? If you haven't, you're in the minority. Prevent this additional frustration for the immediate family by providing a single point of contact within your benefits group. The family can then call that point of contact with any questions or general help in getting medical or death benefits related to the victim. This should be assigned during your planning stages so that the benefits department can be well prepared. The family should also be provided with a single point of contact within the human resource group in order to give any other assistance they need.

EMPLOYEE CARE

Your employees, including the ones not present at the time of the violent act, will be in emotional distress. Counselors should be on-site, or if the facility will not be reopening soon, counselors should be brought into nearby hotel conference rooms to meet with employees. You should encourage your associates to take advantage of these services. Also, the effects of the emotional trauma may not immediately come to the surface, so even those who say that they are fine should be urged to have at least one meeting with a counselor.

Your management and human resource staff should stay close to the employees to determine if they are having psychological problems or do not feel safe working at your facility. In order to deal with their fears, this may also be the time to execute your enhanced security plan.

There are many reasons to keep the news media away from your employees. In the "Public Communication" section, we will cover the emotional effect the media may have on your employees. Many associates will feel uncomfortable with the throng of media trucks and reporters that will be descending on your premises after the event. Some will not want to rehash the events that have just occurred with a throng of reporters. Others will be in emotional trauma and it will be detrimental to their mental health to be approached by the members of the news media. Therefore you will want to let the media know that no one at the location will be talking to them. In most cities, counties, and states, you can keep the media off of your property if you can show law enforcement where the legal boundary lines are located. Again, the time to determine the boundary lines is during your planning stages, not once an event has occurred.

Immediately after the event, inquiries from the media should be referred to the public information officer from the law enforcement agency having jurisdiction over the crime scene.

POLICE RELATIONS

At some point shortly after the police have cleared the building, their investigation will commence. It will be best to set up *points of contact* between your organization and the investigating agency. You will want to have the office and mobile phone numbers for the police department's public information officer and the numbers for a point of contact on the investigation team. As mentioned before, all media inquires should be referred to the public information officer. Any possible newly discovered evidence (e.g. an associate remembers something he or she did not tell the investigators during the official statement) should be forwarded to your investigation contact. The investigating team will want one point of contact to assist them with their needs such as:

- Providing them with the names and contact information for all associates, highlighting those who were on-site at the time of the violent act.
- Helping to ensure that all associates, who were on-site at the time of the incident, have been accounted for and are not injured.
- Access to any personnel or other records as required for their investigation
- Scheduling associate-witness interviews.
- Determining if possible evidence belonged to the business or was brought in by the person who committed the crime (e.g. if a knife was found by the police, they will want to know if it was used in the course of business or if the killer brought the knife onto the premises).
- A complete set of blueprints for the facility. This will help police confirm that they have cleared every part of the facility as well as being able to identify where all of the doors and other possible points of entry are located.
- Access to your closed-circuit surveillance system. Whoever is the most knowledgeable about the system needs to be on call to assist the police. If the data on your surveillance system is encrypted, you will need to have the resources available to decrypt the data for them.

- Information regarding the location of any hazardous, flammable, or ex-plosive material that might be kept on the premises.

Any public statement that your organization is planning to release should be vetted with the investigating agency's public information officer. This is done to insure that any statements supplied to the media do not relate information that the police department does not want made public.

INTERIM BUSINESS RECOVERY

Getting back to business should be a priority after the incident. Undoubtedly there will be a concern about how any business interruption will affect stability of the organization's financials, but this is not a book about business—it is a book about survival and recovery. So let's first focus on the surrounding community and your associates.

Getting back to business is important for both the healing of the community and your employees. The people in the surrounding area will be devastated that such a heinous deed has scarred their community. Seeing your business reopen will help their sense of feeling good about their neighborhood and the businesses in the community. Additionally your employees will very quickly want to get back to work so they can commiserate with their coworkers and return to a sense of normalcy. Everyone should have had several visits with your employee assistance counselors who have helped them overcome their grief and anxiety, readying them for a return to work. There will be those that are reluctant to return and you will probably find that many of them did not follow up with their counseling sessions. This is another reason why it is important to encourage everyone to take advantage of the counseling you are offering. The counselors should also be on hand during the first few days back in business to assist any of the employees who might be feeling any anxiety over returning to work.

But *are* you prepared to carry on if your business is closed as a police crime scene for a few hours, a few days, a few weeks, or a month or longer? The larger or more complex the crime scene, the longer it is going to take for the police to process the evidence and turn the facility back over to you. Your interruption may be even longer if you determine that remodeling the facility would be in the best interest of your returning staff.

Every organization should have a business recovery plan in the event that a hurricane, tornado, or earthquake takes the facility off-line for an extended period of time. After a shooting is another time to execute your business recovery plan. If you have not yet developed one, answering the following questions is a great way to get one started:

- If your main facility is going to be closed for a period of time, do you have a temporary facility that can be used?
- If not, where will employees go to get the business back up and running?
- What job functions can be performed by people working from home?
- How will you provide the information technology infrastructure necessary to do business, including communication systems?
- What supplies will you need in your temporary facility and how can you get them ordered and delivered quickly?
- What items still at the crime scene are necessary for conducting business and how can you replicate them at your interim facility?
- How will you communicate to your employees that they are needed back and tell them where to go and what time to be there?

PUBLIC COMMUNICATION

After an incident has occurred, the news media will respond to your facility. It is important to understand that their job is to get a good story on the air. Here's what you can expect:

- They will want a company representative to go on camera and give a statement.
- They will try to approach your employees as they leave the building to get on-camera statements.
- They may show up at the homes of the victims or the victim's families to get them to appear on camera.
- They may want an exclusive interview with a company executive.

If you do not make a statement to the news media, it may get turned into an issue; for example, the story could read, "The company is keeping mum about what happened. They have not returned our numerous calls." Suddenly the fact that you haven't made a statement becomes the story, which may be perceived as if your company has something to hide.

You also want to avoid creating an adversarial relationship with the news media. Respond to their calls, treat them with courtesy and respect, and be open and honest about which topics you can discuss.

Statement Preparation

If your company does not have an experienced media relations representative, then you should hire a reputable public relations firm. As always, it is best to develop this relationship before you actually need them.

Your company should have a policy forbidding employees from talking to the news media or providing them with any policy manuals, video recordings (either from the company closed-circuit TV system or from their personal smartphone), and so forth. The employees need to understand that these actions could be detrimental to law enforcement's investigation of the incident. After an incident occurs, the employees should be reminded that all media requests must be referred to your media relations representative.

Statements should be drafted by your communications or media relations groups and vetted with your public relations firm, legal counsel, and the police department's public information officer. The law enforcement agency must be made aware that you are going to give a statement to the news media and be given the opportunity to vet the information to insure that details crucial to the investigation will not be divulged to the public.

If a senior company executive is going to give the statement, the news media should be informed that the executive will not be taking any questions. Senior executives often feel that they should answer the media's questions, however, they are usually not well prepared. This can cause negative perceptions that should be avoided.

What Should Be in the Company Statement

- The following should always be in the company statement to the press:
  - Expressions of sympathy for the victims and their families
  - Explanations of services or benefits that the company is providing such as:
    - Counseling services for your employees as well as the families of the victims
    - Victim and family financial assistance or trust fund arrangements
  - Expressions of appreciation to the law enforcement and the emergency service agencies who have responded
- The following *should not* be in the statement to the press:
  - Information or commentary regarding law enforcement's investigation
  - Discussions about liability for the incident

Handling Questions

All questions relating to the incident and the investigation should be referred to the law enforcement public information officer with this disclaimer: "It would be inappropriate for us to comment while this matter is under investigation by the authorities."

The media may ask your representative a question about a political issue, such as "Do you think this would have happened if the legislature had passed the tougher gun laws that were proposed last year?" These types of questions are designed to provide a controversial sound bite for the next newscast and can polarize public opinion toward your company. We recommend that you avoid a direct response and say something along these lines: "Right now we are focused on the victims and their families, and speculating on the impact that some proposed public policy may or may not have had is not something that I can address."

Requests for Exclusive Interviews

We do not recommend giving exclusive interviews for the following reasons:
- If you do not provide every media outlet the same opportunity, you may make enemies at a time when you do not need any aggravation from the press.
- Your interview will be edited, spliced, and possibly aired with your comments taken out of context. You should only consider exclusive interviews if:
  - There is a specific and important message that needs to be communicated to the public.
  - The news organization grants you approval over how they edit and comment on the interview. This is very tough but a good public relations firm can help negotiate these points with the news organization.

Helping Victims and Their Families Deal with the News Media

Victims and/or their families may turn to you for assistance if they have been contacted for an interview by the news media. In order to protect against the perception that you are influencing their statements, it is best to refer them to their own attorney.

The information presented in this chapter has been intended to be as inclusive as we can make it, but you must choose what to do based on the situation with which you are dealing. Also remember, even as we discuss these topics in sequential order, the preassigned people or functions need to begin executing all components as soon as possible.

AFTERWORD BY DAN MURPHY

First meetings can leave lasting impressions. It was in October 2004 in an office of a Fortune 100 company where I first met Randy Ferris. I was in town meeting with senior leaders of the company, discussing a position with the organization. Randy was already the Director of Loss Prevention, running a large, well-established, successful team that spanned 47 states. What was supposed to be a simple, quick introduction resulted in a lengthy discussion of the nature of disturbing and harassing behavior. This was the result of a morbid painting that hung on the wall of Randy's office directly behind his desk. The painting, it turned out, had been sent by an anonymous individual to the company's CEO and contained a mix of disturbing images and dates of violent tragedies, such as Hitler's invasion of Poland, the assignation of President Kennedy, and the Columbine High School shootings. Randy recounted how the painting was sent and talked a bit about the other types of odd and at times, threatening, correspondence that was commonly received at the company. It was soon clear that we shared a common interest in the investigation of such activities and of developing a deeper understanding of the psychology of the individuals who engage in threatening and stalking behavior such as this. After about an hour, we parted and I returned home to ponder the job offer that followed his visit.

Soon after I accepted the offer we began partnering on the assessment and management of all threatening and disturbing behavior reported within the company. Randy had recently inaugurated the company's first Violence Prevention Plan that trained managers and supervisors to report threats and instances of disturbing behavior to the Loss Prevention or Human Resource departments. At first, some of the cases were fairly routine and threat management plans were easily devised and executed, but other cases were more complex and, quite frankly, rather unsettling. We continued our threat management education and continued to update our violence prevention programs with what we learned. During these times we also ran up against the rationalizations, objections, and denials, or RODS, as discussed early in the book, and learned how to overcome them.

Taking our collective decades of relevant experience, and a shared passion for protecting people we created Violence Prevention Strategies LLC in 2013. This idea was born out of the many requests we were receiving to speak at events and requests from companies asking if we could help them build a program for their organizations. Many of those were small to midsize companies with little in the way of infrastructure or capability in this area. Since then, we have helped many organizations create effective, reasonable programs to ensure the proper management of cases involving threatening and disturbing behavior. We also frequently receive calls from client companies who need help managing a specific threat. We provide guidance and support to help them manage the situation to a peaceful resolution.

When the opportunity presented itself to write this book, we knew we would be challenged in selecting which of the many thousands of cases we have handled or studied to illustrate in the book. These cases have ranged from the boring to the bizarre and everything in between. Those we chose to discuss highlight particular points that we hope have helped to bring to life the concepts and best practices detailed in this book. It is our sincere hope that those who read this book will learn something they did not know or had not thought about with regards to dealing with those who threaten or display disturbing or harassing behavior. We hope it will spark discussions in workplaces and help bring about the development of effective, reasonable, defendable programs designed to protect people by preventing violence. We both have dedicated our professional lives to that end.

SUBJECT INDEX

Printed in the United States
By Bookmasters